Super Network of Corruption in Venezuela

Kleptocracy, Nepotism and Human Rights Violation

Eduardo Salcedo-Albarán
Luis Jorge Garay-Salamanca
Authors

José Ugaz Sánches-Moreno
Foreword

To each victim.

Contents

Warning

In the case of the names mentioned, cited or referred to in this text, of people accused or indicted but who have not yet been judicially convicted, the presumption of innocence is preserved as a guarantee of individual rights and due process. Judicial truth is jurisdiction of the courts, which, by law, will decide whether the accused are innocent or guilty.

Therefore, it is clarified that appearing in an interaction such as "to be the last beneficiary of", "to be a member of", "being connected to" or, in general, showing up on a network such as those analyzed herein, does not necessarily imply committing an illegal act or being involved in a criminal enterprise by active agency. It is always possible that an individual, despite promoting legal and lawful activities, "belongs to", "participates in", "is connected to" or appears in an illicit network as a result of coercion or deception, or due to failures in the preliminary processes of judicial investigations, or for any other reason not related to the commission of criminal acts.

The analysis presented in this book is primarily based on judicial information from different jurisdictions that complement journalistic sources, so, except for some specific cases, most individuals and companies mentioned herein as members of the structure of "Super network of corruption in Venezuela" still lack judicial sentence and are protected by the formal presumption of innocence.

Foreword

Venezuela is an open wound for humanity. Unfortunately, it shares this condition with other countries that, as a result of war and violence, are struggling in severe humanitarian crises, such as Syria, South Sudan or Somalia. The difference between these and Venezuela is that the humanitarian tragedy suffered by the latter is almost exclusively the result of one factor: corruption, or as this book shows us, the so-called macro-corruption, and its acknowledged institutional co-optation.

Many believe that Venezuela's problems are due to a failed ideological model expressed in the Hugo Chávez' heroic creation: "Bolivarianism". Chávez, a former military man who came to power after a failed coup attempt, installed a totalitarian dictatorship inspired supposedly by leftist dogmas, which has survived and subsists to date, even though many predicted that it would not survive after its creator's departure.

I do not share that vision. What has happened in Venezuela since 1998, when Chávez won the elections, is the mounting of a cruel and organized kleptocracy whose government plan consists of looting the country for the exclusive benefit of those at the top of the regime. These characters, civilians and military, have enriched themselves to unbelievable levels, while millions of Venezuelans suffer from hunger and deprivation of their basic subsistence rights, being condemned to malnutrition, diseases and, in many cases, death, or, if lucky enough to avoid this, forced to migrate in absolutely precarious conditions.

The last time I visited Venezuela was at the end of 2019. I had the opportunity to interview and interact with many people who gave me their opinions about the situation in the country, and they were kind enough, not without fear in many cases, to share with me valuable information and experiences.

I must confess that, on more than one occasion, I felt chills down my spine as I listened, incredulous at first, moved later, at the both heartbreaking and outrageous stories of my interlocutors. Such was my impact those days, that as soon as I settled on the return plane, I felt the need to write what I had experienced and heard. Now I share with you some of these notes:

"In terms of citizen security, Venezuela has become the country with the highest levels of violence in the world. A year

into the Chávez government, in 2003, homicides went up from 4,000 to 8,000. Today, 15 years later, in Venezuela 28,000 homicides are committed per year, which is equivalent to 91.8 homicides per 100,000 inhabitants, a figure unmatched in the world.

This accelerated deterioration of internal security is due to the fact that, shortly after coming to power, the regime distorted the public security system. Then, in a perverse logic, organized crime was instrumentalized to reinforce some of the regime's practices and to orchestrate violent responses against dissent.

The institutional dismantling has reached such an extreme that two policemen are murdered each day in Caracas nowadays. The police are scarce (there's a 200% deficit), poorly paid, and it lack incentives (a commissioner with 20 years of experience earns a symbolic salary of US $15 a month). Since 2015, the so-called "Operations for the Liberation of the People" (OLP, or "Operaciones de Liberación del Pueblo"), which are uncontrolled raids on the protection of human rights that have caused more than 550 deaths to date.

The regime has created the sinister and all-powerful SEBIN (Servicio Bolivariano de Inteligencia Nacional, or "Bolivarian National Intelligence Service"). In its dungeons (El Helicoide and La Tumba), there are more than 300 political prisoners that have been detained there for years, without charge, without trial, subjected to torture and without any type of control. Fully subordinated judges and prosecutors do not process habeas corpus nor are they authorized to enter.

In economic matters, Venezuela imports 90% of what it needs (it buys between US$ 35,000 and US$ 45,000 million in food a year). It has an unpayable debt with China (US$ 44,000 million) and Russia (US$ 20,000 million), where the total debt went from US$ 30,000 million to US$ 300,000 million. Inflation reached 2,000,000%.

The Government has created a currency exchange system that generates great distortions and has made corrupt fortunes possible with the abuse of the preferential exchange rate (10 vs. 24,000 bolivars per dollar).

The productive apparatus of the country has been destroyed. In 1978, Venezuela produced 75% of its food; today it produces only 5%. Food distribution has been handed over to the military, creating a huge corrupt market for speculation through the so-called "bachaqueros" and the resale of stolen food from the Local Popular Supply Committees (CLAP, or "Comités Locales de Abastecimiento Popular"), a distribution system for the market food basket that has also become an inexhaustible source of corrupt structures to favor government authorities and business partners, capturing millions of dollars as a result of food surcharges.

The shortage of food and medicine has created a humanitarian crisis in the country: 82% of the population lives in extreme poverty (94% of Venezuelans do not have enough income to pay for the market food basket), and 61% only eat twice a day, with an average per capita weight loss of 11 kg. since the beginning of the crisis. There are 4 million malnourished Venezuelans: 33% of children at low-income social sectors suffer from growth retardation. Approximately 1,500,000 children between the ages of 0 and 2 are chronically malnourished. Over 400,000 children require immediate attention to avoid irreversible damage and thousands die, due to lack of adequate medical care.

In recent years, over 4 million people have emigrated out of a population of 31 million and 700,000 children have dropped out of school.

On the other hand, PDVSA, the once giant and powerful state oil company, has become the spoils of the regime. The company is devastated. Chávez laid off over 20,000 workers and then tripled the payroll with people that belongs to the regime. To date, despite the dramatic drop in production due to inefficiency, 100% of the foreign exchange that Venezuela receives comes from the sale of oil, having lost US$ 31,000 million due to gasoline smuggling in the last decade.

There has been a total co-optation of the institutions by the regime: The Supreme Court, the General Comptroller's Office, the General Prosecutor's Office, the Central Bank of Venezuela, among others.

Among the many corruption scandals, there are the Money Flight case in which an embezzlement of US$ 1,200 million was detected, the case of the construction company Conkor involving Tarek William Saab (Attorney General appointed by the Constituent Assembly), and Odebrecht's, a Brazilian company that is now famous for corruption across Latin America and that has been paid over US$ 20,000 million, despite there being no ongoing investigation against it in Venezuela. It is estimated that between 2002 and 2015, US$ 120,000 million have been diverted through corruption (only 5 cases of corruption abroad add up to US$ 15,000 million).

To corruption itself, must be added the problem of international drug trafficking and its alliance with the regime. As informed by traditional and social media, drug cartels use the Venezuelan territory as a center of operations with the approval and enrichment, through illegal funds, of the government and its main leaders, several of whom currently appear in the lists of the most wanted drug traffickers in the United States.

This is not about a failed revolution or an incompetent regime. There is a civil-military criminal network in power that has deliberately dismantled the country's productive infrastructure and created corrupt mechanisms to control food, gasoline, and foreign exchange, to generate a black market in which they have become fabulously enriched at the cost of the life and health of the population. The socialist utopia has been buried under tons of corruption."

If now, a year later, I had to modify something of what was written at the end of 2019, only the figures would change, which unfortunately have increased exponentially for the worse.

A colossal tragedy requires an effort of equal magnitude to be understood. This is what this magnificent book that Eduardo Salcedo-Albarán and Luis Jorge Garay-Salamanca present to us today with their renowned technique applied to the analysis of complex criminal networks. Given the dimensions and complexity of the criminal structure implemented in Venezuela, it would not have been possible to pick a better title: "Super Corruption Network in Venezuela". Everything is superlative in this case: the amount stolen, the impudence with which they act, and the impunity they enjoy. It is with good reason that, as the authors point out, there is no precedent in terms of the size and impact of this network expressed in over 17,000 interactions established by 5,000 nodes/agents.

Restraining myself from overextending more than I should, nor "spoiling" your experience as you read this book, I would like to highlight some points that seem particularly relevant to me.

One of the characteristics of the Venezuelan super network is the internationalization of the effects of corruption. To date, there are 85 processes happening against Venezuelan members linked to it in various jurisdictions around the world, for crimes of money laundering, drug trafficking and corruption. This means that, in a global world, a global effort is required to counteract it, recover diverted assets and do justice.

Another relevant element is the power concentration of the macro-network in a few actors. Maduro concentrates 75% of the direct interactions that it establishes (hub) as an issuing agent, and also has the highest indicator as a structural bridge in network flows (betweenness).

He is joined by a few more (José Cabello Rondón, Tareck Zaidan El Aisami Maddah, Diosdado Cabello Rondón, among others). In total, 10 nodes/agents concentrate 52.5 of the betweenness indicator. This is very important from the perspective of deactivating the network, because it means that, by neutralizing a small number of key actors, the macro-corruption structure can be dismantled.

From a victimology perspective, the structural impunity that the co-opted justice system guarantees poses a great challenge when considering the transition process that will inevitably come when the Maduro regime collapses. From this point of view, the approach to define who is a victim of acts of macro-corruption is very intriguing. The legal tradition has held for years that, since corruption affects the legal asset referred to as "public administration", those who suffer its consequences are "the people" or "society" as a whole, judicially represented by the State; however, defining the individual and collective victims of this catastrophe will also be inevitable.

The book raises the importance of repairing the victims of corruption, as an essential right in the context of restoring personal and institutional trust to lay the foundations for rebuilding democracy. This will demand creative thinking, detached from formalism, to find solutions typical of the dynamic of transitional justice, in which reparations focus on individuals, and not only on representative groups of the "social damage". These solutions should include patrimonial and extra-patrimonial compensations, such as anamnestic justice (based on the memory recovery), which includes symbolic events and gestures of remediation for the achievement of the necessary structural transformations that the democratic transition will require.

In short, this is an indispensable reading book to understand the new trends in corrupt criminality developed by macro-networks, and from there, to outline alternative solutions for a phenomenon that is devastating for humanity, as the case of Venezuela shows.

Jose C. Ugaz SM.

I. Introduction

As in most of Latin America, corruption is not new in Venezuela; in fact, death penalty to punish corruption has been decreed since 1813 by Simón Bolívar "in the first republic of Venezuela" (Coronel, 2006, p. 2). However, during the second decade of the 21st century, Venezuela has become the most serious case of corruption not only at the region but possibly worldwide; this seriousness is reflected in the complexity of its structures and in the magnitude of the public resources compromised. In this sense, although corruption is not new in Venezuela, its current levels are, reaching an advanced stage of macro-corruption and institutional co-optation (Garay Salamanca, Salcedo-Albarán, & Macías, 2018d) with unprecedented impacts.

The macro nature of corruption in Venezuela results of the complexity and scale of the corruption network discussed in this book, and which is reflected in the high diversity and number of nodes/agents involved, as well as their established interactions. This complexity allows defining the resulting network as a macro-network, that is, a structure that meets the quantitative complexity criteria necessary to be defined as macro (Salcedo-Albarán & Garay-Salamanca, 2016). In fact, the macro-corruption and institutional co-optation network in Venezuela analyzed herein consists of more than 5,000 nodes/agents that established over 17,000 interactions; a magnitude that lacks previous reference worldwide and exceeds the magnitude of macro-networks of corruption previously analyzed by the authors. As a result, the network here analyzed is defined as a super network of corruption and co-optation, especially to draw attention to its high level of complexity. In fact, this super network even exceeds the magnitude size of networks already defined as complex networks or super networks (Li, Hu, Song, Yang, & Li, 2019). As discussed in chapter 5, the large magnitude of this super network is evident, for example, when it is compared to the Lava Jato macro-corruption network originating in Brazil, which has been considered until now as the largest case of systemic corruption in the world (Garay Salamanca, Salcedo-Albarán, & Macías, 2018d).

In this book it is presented and discussed the first empirical analysis of the network of macro-corruption and institutional co-optation that affects the Venezuelan State. This super structure, articulated by numerous individuals, entities, and public institutions, condemns Venezuelan society to a complex humanitarian emergency accompanied by the worst economic, political and social crisis in the Americas in the face of "the intensified political landscape, food and medicine shortages, and increased crime rate and institutional weakness" (Transparencia Venezuela, 2017).

To develop the illicit network model presented herein, concepts, methods and protocols of criminal networks analysis were applied. This framework has been defined and developed since the beginning of the decade to understand characteristics of macro-corruption networks, such as: (i) the number and types of nodes/agents involved, (ii) the number and types of interactions established, (iii) the relevant nodes/agents that can be interpreted as potentially most responsible during corruption, institutional cooptation and victimization processes, and (iv) the characteristics of the component subnetworks of the super-network (Garay Salamanca & Salcedo-Albarán, 2012; Garay Salamanca, Salcedo-Albarán, & Macías, 2018d).

The criminal network analysis approach used here is theoretically based on social network analysis (Degenne & Forsé, 1999; Carrington, Scoot, & Wasserman, 2005; Csermely, 2006; Borgatti, Mehra, Brass, & Labianca, 2009), and it has been applied since a decade ago to analyze Co-opted State Reconfiguration processes carried out by small and extensive illicit networks, especially in terms of their institutional effects (Garay-Salamanca, Salcedo-Albarán, & Beltrán, 2010a, 2010b; Garay-Salamanca & Salcedo-Albarán, 2012a). These initial analyses were based on theoretical and methodological developments in which basic applications of social network analysis were used to study criminal networks (Morselli C., 2008), such as arms trafficking (Morselli C., 2012).

Criminal networks analysis has been applied to model and analyze corruption structures at regional, national, and transnational levels in Colombia, Mexico, Peru, Guatemala, and Brazil (Garay-Salamanca, Salcedo-Albarán, & Duarte, 2017; Garay Salamanca & Salcedo-Albarán, 2012; Garay Salamanca, Salcedo-Albarán, & Macías, 2018d; Salcedo-Albarán *et al*, 2019; Salcedo-Albarán & Garay-Salamanca, 2019g). Other analyzed cases include, for instance, trafficking networks of rhino horn (Goga, Goredema, & Salcedo-Albarán, 2017), pangolin (Hübschle, 2017), organs (Salcedo-Albarán & Santos, 2017), and minerals (Lopez & Salcedo-Albarán, 2017).

Based on these cases, the concept of macro-corruption and institutional co-optation has been defined as a process characterized *"by the systemic, planned and coordinated participation of multiple agents that can be (i) public and private, (ii) individuals and organizations such as private companies, and (iii) legal, illegal or 'gray', to carry out various actions, activities, relationships or agreements (that) usually involve the manipulation of rules and procedures, such as public procurement processes, money laundering through national and transnational financial operations (...), not only to obtain short-term profits, but also to co-opt institutions and establish stable relationships with political parties and their leaders through the financing of electoral campaigns, for instance, with the consequent selection, cooperation and strategic permanence of certain high-ranking public officials in state companies and key public institutions",* to ensure the permanence of the scheme for the co-optation of public processes such as public procurement.

In addition, due to the development of robust computational tools, the concept of macro-criminal networks or macro-criminality networks has been defined as the *"(...) criminal network that exceeds by two orders of magnitude the approximate maximum number of nodes (...) that a human can identify and memorize in a social network"* (Salcedo-Albarán & Garay-Salamanca, 2016). However, as shown herein, a super structure such as that of Venezuela exceeds the previously modeled and analyzed macro-corruption networks by several orders of magnitude.

The super network of macro-corruption analyzed in this book was modeled by reviewing official and media sources from different countries, due to two reasons. First: due to the serious situation of institutional weakness, corruption, and generalized impunity in the Venezuelan justice system (United Nations, Human Rights Office of the High Commissioner, 2018), investigations, processes and trials carried out within the country are scarce. Second: due to the extent of the macro-corruption network, and its connection to transnational crimes such as drug trafficking, the agents involved have established money laundering schemes around the world; therefore, there are currently over 85 judicial processes against Venezuelans for charges of money laundering, corruption, or drug trafficking in various international jurisdictions (Transparencia Venezuela, 2019). To this extent, the official sources consulted consisted of a few judicial records produced in Venezuela and, mainly, documents produced by prosecutors in other countries where legal proceedings are being carried out against Venezuelan citizens, as well as reports and records from state bodies. Similarly, media sources were consulted in those countries where investigations and legal proceedings are being carried out against Venezuelan citizens, as well as to a few independent portals that still exist in Venezuela despite the repression exerted by the regime.

The sources were systematized by a team of analysts and consolidated in an interactions database (IdB), following protocols and algorithms developed by Fundación Vortex (Vortex Foundation & SciVortex Corp., 2020), and by using the Analysis of Criminal Networks Vortex Platform 1.0 (PARCV 1.0). This IdB, subject to permanent review and expansion, contains a set of interactions that informs how the nodes/agents identified in the macro-corruption network interacted from the year 2000 to the beginning of 2020. Then, with the IdB, the illicit network model and the visualizations were drawn up. These visualizations consist of points (nodes/agents) that represent natural or legal persons, public or private, as well as arrows that represent interactions with a specific direction. Therefore, in each of the 17,000 interactions compiled in the IdB, the following elements are identified: (i) the active or issuing node/agent, (ii) the passive or receiving node/agent, (iii) the type of interaction established, and (iv) the public source that supports the interaction.

Once the model was developed, two centrality indicators were calculated to identify the most relevant nodes/agents of the network: (i) the direct centrality indicator, which informs the percentage proportion of direct interactions in which each node/agent of the network participates, and (ii) the indicator of intervention or betweenness that informs the percentage proportion of indirect routes in which each node/agent intervenes (Degenne & Forsé, 1999; Carrington, Scoot, &

Wasserman, 2005). These two indicators allow to identify those nodes/agents that exercised, or still exercise, a relevant articulating role for the super network to operate. In fact, registering a high indicator of direct centrality and betweenness, and therefore being a relevant articulator of the network, is a necessary – but not sufficient – criterion for a node/agent to be interpreted as bearing the greatest responsible in the processes of victimization observed in the network. In Venezuela, as in other countries where advanced processes of institutional co-optation are registered, these nodes/agents can simultaneously be considered among the most responsible in networks of macro-corruption and macro-victimization.

This book consists of 6 chapters. After this introduction, the second chapter is a brief recount of the socioeconomic, political, and institutional context in which the current corruption processes registered in Venezuela take place. This chapter does not specify the historical, social, political and economic causes of the current problematic situation, it only reviews some antecedents identified by other specialized authors to understand it. In this sense, these reference elements are discussed to facilitate analyzing the current situation.

In the third chapter the main characteristics of the super network of macro-corruption and institutional co-optation in Venezuela are exposed, as well as the characteristics of the nodes/agents with the highest centrality indicators and that, therefore, act as hubs and structural bridges of the super network. This chapter also presents and analyzes the characteristics of four subnetworks that are part of the analyzed structure – corruption, violation of human rights, macro-corruption in the food sector and in the oil sector – and of the most important nodes/agents in each one.

In the fourth chapter, the geodesic routes that indirectly connect some relevant nodes/agents with Nicolás Maduro, who is the structural bridge and hub of the super network, are analyzed. As it will be seen, some relevant nodes/agents strategically manage valuable resources minimizing the number of direct interactions and maximizing the number of geodesic routes, by interacting with other strategic nodes/agents. For this analysis, the stealth indicator is proposed and calculated for a set of analyzed nodes/agents, which reports on the ratio between the total number of geodesic routes and the number of direct interactions for each node/agent.

In the fifth chapter, the characteristics of the super network of macro-corruption and institutional co-optation in Venezuela are compared with the characteristics of the *Lava Jato* macro-network, to illustrate the unprecedented magnitude of the public budget affected in the former case.

The sixth chapter presents some implications and challenges that Venezuelan society will surely face as it seeks to rebuild and legitimize its public institutions after the current crisis. As discussed, the economic damages are not the only ones neither the main results of the super network of macro-corruption in Venezuela, but perhaps the institutional and humanitarian ones. Given that this super network of macro-corruption has no antecedents in studied cases, the massive victimization deriving from it will surely have no antecedents either. Therefore, identifying and repairing individual, collective and social victims will be one of the main challenges that Venezuelan society will face in its quest to establish a modern, inclusive and democratic rule of law. For this reason, the post scriptum presents some explorative ideas for comprehensively repairing victims of corruption in the health sector.

II. Some Background: From Chávez to Maduro

An essential factor to understand the situation of corruption in Venezuela, that perhaps has aggravated it, is the concentration of the largest oil reserves in the world. Coinciding with the outstanding magnitude of revenues that Venezuela has received by exploiting hydrocarbons, it is possible that the extent of corruption registered in the country is unparalleled in other countries, especially in the developing world. Thus, despite the hydrocarbon reserves in Venezuela, with 298 billion barrels as of January 2015, this is currently one of the weakest and most collapsed economies in the world (Kumar, Toshniwal, & Gupta, 2016), and scene of the most complex crisis in Latin America, characterized by food shortages, political instability, and hyperinflation (Mejía, 2018).

Dependence on oil revenues and the opacity in the management of public resources have dramatically stimulated corruption. According to Mejía (2018), this dependence on oil revenues, which supports the definition of Venezuela as a "Petro-State", was consolidated in 1958 during Marco Pérez Jiménez' transition from the military dictatorship to a democracy, and the celebration of the *"Pacto de Punto Fijo"* (Fixed Point Pact) between the representatives of the main political parties at that time. Then, during the 1970s, the military and diplomatic crises in the Middle East led to a boom in international oil prices, so revenues tripled in Venezuela. However, this boom was not accompanied by rigorous institutional and administrative control instruments, but rather by a "dramatic" deterioration in the administration of the country's assets, to the point that during the first term of Carlos Andrés Pérez, Venezuela had approximately 300 financially unviable state companies (Coronel, 2006, p. 2). As a result, by the end of the 1970s the public debt of the Venezuelan State increased despite its high income. However, authors such as Mejía (2018) acknowledge that this period was also characterized by sustained economic growth, strengthening of political parties and relative democratic governance.

Contrary to the 1970s, the decade of the 1980s was characterized by political polarization, lower economic growth, and a weakening of the democratic governance. The collapse of the *"Punto Fijo"* would then open the path for social discontent that Chávez later took advantage of to promote his political project, namely: Bolivarianism, which channeled the rejection of the *"puntofijismo"* (Mejía, 2018, p. 44).

At the beginning of this century, the rise of international oil prices did not translate into institutional or administrative strengthening of Venezuela; in fact, it was reflected by disorderly and fragmented social spending without increasing of productivity or social welfare, which ultimately led to inefficiency, corruption, and a significant increase in public debt (Kumar, Toshniwal, & Gupta, 2016). Then, the arrival of Hugo Chávez to power in 1999 accentuated the situation of corruption that had been deteriorating since the 1970s, even though one of the three pillars of his campaign was to "eradicate corruption", along with "writing a new constitution", and "to fight against social exclusion and poverty". These Chávez proposals were accepted by a country whose population was suffering "60% poverty and 30% extreme poverty" (Coronel, 2006, p. 4).

"Chavism": Deepening Opacity

During the first 7 years of the Chávez administration, the government received between USD\$175 and USD\$225 billion from oil income and new debt, while public transparency and accountability was drastically reduced. For example, the Venezuelan oil company PDVSA stopped publishing financial statements in 2003, and oil transfers became a discretionary executive decision (Coronel, 2006). For this reason, although during the second decade of this century PDVSA announced the development of external audits, there have been permanent *"inconsistencies between the annual data and those estimated by international agencies"* (Kumar, Toshniwal, & Gupta, 2016, p. 16).

Capitalizing on social discontent and counting on abundant economic resources, Chávez initiated reforms to dismantle, transform and control key institutions such as the National Congress, the Supreme Court of Justice, and the Electoral Council (Coronel, 2006). However, despite these reforms and the supposed break with "traditional politics", several structural anomalies remained unchanged at the political and social levels, such as the selective, concentrating and excluding distribution of income, the renewal and reallocation of privileges within of the country's elites, as well as the high dependence on oil income. In this sense, despite his revolutionary discourse, Chávez's political project was not structurally distant from traditional political and institutional malpractices (Mejía, 2018). Since the beginning Chávez quickly expressed little interest in consolidating institutions; for instance, after his arrival, he threatened the Supreme Court of Justice for not deciding in accordance with the purposes of his so-called "revolution" and promoted 33 army officers without the approval of the Senate, contrary to the provisions of Article 150 of the National Constitution (Coronel, 2006).

The above happened behind an apparent proclaimed anti-corruption discourse. In November, 1999, the then Minister of Foreign Affairs, José Vicente Rangel, stated in a public speech that eradicating corruption and having a reliable judicial system were fundamental objectives of the "revolution" initiated by Chávez, although, in practice, none of those commitments turned into actions.

In fact, the anti-corruption discourse was combined with outstanding discretion and opacity in the management of oil resources and public resources in general. The large transfers registered in 2005 and 2006 to the National Development Fund, FONDEN, established by presidential decree in 2005, and to the development bank established in 2001, BANDES, entities that reported only to the president, failed to comply with the adopted regulations and provisions almost since the beginning (Coronel, 2006). As a result of permanent discretion in transfers from PDVSA to FONDEN, the fund failed to fulfill its purpose of stabilizing the economy (Kumar, Toshniwal, & Gupta, 2016), while an economic reserve fund was not established with oil revenues. These failures reinforced the weak institutional framework and the extractive and unproductive economic model currently observed in Venezuela (Mejía, 2018, p. 46).

The rigorous and transparent operation of stabilizing funds nourished with oil revenues has been essential to avoid economic crises in countries with high dependence on natural resources; in fact, the strict administration of these funds has defined the difference between economic failure or success: "between the blessing or the curse" of the availability of natural resources. Specifically, preventing the executive branch from transferring money directly from the central bank has been a critical condition to avoid increasing fiscal deficit and its corresponding effects on inflation and the revaluation of the currency in countries with high oil revenues (Kumar, Toshniwal, & Gupta, 2016). These restrictions and the rigorous administration of stabilization funds explain why a country like Norway, which registers an abundance of hydrocarbons, has a domestic economy relatively independent from the severe fluctuations in international oil prices (Kumar, Toshniwal, & Gupta, 2016).[1]

In contrast, the management of stabilization funds in Venezuela has been characterized by discretion and opacity.

____

[1] For instance, the Global Government Pension Fund of Norway, originally known as Government Pension Fund, was established in 1990 to transfer, concentrate and manage oil revenues. After fulfilling rigorous and transparent conditions, if there is any deficit during a fiscal year, it is deducted from the fund (Kumar, Toshniwal, & Gupta, 2016).

In fact, the public administration of Venezuela in general has been characterized by irregular or technically unjustified decisions during the last two decades, which has reflected on: (i) the central government transferring unjustified resources *"to buy off political loyalties in the region to consolidate their political project"* (Coronel, 2006, p. 6), (ii) unjustified transfer of gold reserves from the Central Bank, apparently by Chávez's direct orders, (iii) modification of the Central Bank regulations to allow direct and unconditional transfers towards the executive branch, (iv) financial privileges in the form of loans and purchase of bonds in favor of banks in countries that supported Chávez's political project, (v) development of public procurement processes without due bidding requirements, (vi) approximate expenditure of USD$17 billion in discretionary arms purchases to Spain and Russia, as well as transfers to countries in Latin America and the Caribbean to secure support at the United Nations Security Council, (vii) financing and execution of social programs lacking budgetary control and characterized by false billing and irregular contracts, especially those developed by the Military Forces, such as "Bolívar 2000" led by Commander Víctor Cruz Weffer, or the "United Social Fund" led by Commander William Fariñas, Chávez's partner during the 1992 coup attempt, (viii) irregular acquisition of the presidential plane for USD$ 65 million, violating article 314 of the National Constitution and other budgetary regulations, and (ix) agreements such as the one signed in 2000 to supply oil to Cuba for 15 years, characterized by irregularities such as Cuba re-exporting a portion of the supplied oil, and delays in payments of approximately USD$1.3 billion a year. These decisions without due technical support, sometimes backed by laws approved and tailored to favor corrupt interests, are added to other even more structural ones, which have led to the collapse of the country's energy, infrastructure, and health systems.

Some authors identify three types of corruption that converge in Venezuela around the irregular management of oil resources: (i) "Great Corruption" at the design and implementation levels of public policy, (ii) corruption in the operation of the bureaucratic apparatus, and (iii) *systemic corruption in relationships between government officials and private agents*" (Kumar, Toshniwal, & Gupta, 2016, p. 17). In this context, the distribution of public resources obeys the objective of legitimizing the government and strengthening its clientelism networks, usually lacking the minimum criteria of integrity, transparency, or accountability. This has led to "*a large part of the oil revenues being used discretionally and without any transparency. Increasing corruption, foreign exchange operations, and extralegal activities such as smuggling offer significant opportunities for personal gain and [political] group building*" (Peters, 2017, pp. 56-57).

Clientelism, due to institutional deterioration, has accentuated in Venezuela since the failed referendum of 2004, when the Government took advantage of large amounts of resources from oil revenues to pay for political favors (Mejía, 2018). These clientelistic criteria in the distribution of public resources do not result of a true substantive democracy, but rather from a formal one usually supported by widely questioned electoral processes. In the framework of this formal democracy, public policies have the main purpose of seeking the survival of the government and are, therefore, directed to favor allied sectors (Garay Salamanca, Salcedo-Albarán, & Álvarez Villa, 2020; Hepp, 2019).

Since it came to power, Chavism has granted public positions to a few relatives and close friends of the president and high-ranking officials. From these positions, there is a privileged access to decisions regarding the allocation of State resources to sustain the political power of the ruling party and to secure exclusive private benefit for some privileged agents. As a result, nepotism, clientelism, and the militarization of the politics and the economy currently conduct to embezzling public funds, reproducing illegal activities such as drug trafficking, and creating façade companies for money laundering purposes, among other illicit activities (López Maya, 2018, p. 76).

On the other hand, the overwhelming government interference has negatively affected Venezuelan economic productivity, since the country's productive activities are also permeated by clientelist criteria (Sutherland, 2018). The economic mismanagement by the Government has even slowed down the productivity of sectors such as agriculture, and the production of iron, steel, and cement, among others (Sutherland, 2018, p. 143; Vera, 2018, p. 92). In addition, this scheme has fostered the enrichment of a bureaucratic-military sector usually referred to as *"Boliburguesía"* (Bolivarian Bourgeoisie), which has taken advantage of its control of key economic and political positions, among others to obtain private benefit (Sutherland, 2018) through the configuration of systemic institutional co-optation structures; this explains why the main corruption cases known usually involve clientelism and decisive participation of the military.

By assigning key decision-making positions to militaries who lack technical qualifications, the regime has secured support and loyalty from this sector, while opening wide opportunities for corruption. This situation has resulted in military leaders benefiting *"from corruption and the administration of public resources as a form of control"* (Puerta Riera, 2017, p. 176). As discussed below, this situation affects various economic activities, from the distribution of food, the administration of customs and taxes, to the allocation of oil revenues, the iron industry, and other mining industries.

Simultaneously, the de-professionalization of Military Forces and the establishment of a "Praetorian State" have increased an exaggerated autonomy of the military branch, compared to the civil power and, therefore, this has diminished the possibility of accountability and democratic control to their actions (Jácome, 2017). In addition to the mismanagement of economic sectors in which large public budgets are misused, some military personnel have participated in drug trafficking and transnational organized crime activities, such as smuggling and human trafficking, mainly at the border with Colombia (Jácome, 2017). Additionally, due to their privileges in accessing foreign preferential currencies for international trade transactions, some military personnel have created "façade companies" to carry out fictitious or overvalued imports (Lander & Arconada, 2017). Thus, the administrative and discretionary manipulation of preferential foreign exchange rates has become a recurring corrupt scheme to extract large amounts of public resources (Transparencia Venezuela, 2019).

"Madurism": Consolidating Macro-corruption and Human Rights Violation

Chávez's death on March 5, 2013, left Venezuela immersed in a regime that maintained some practices of *"puntofijismo"*, such as economic dependence on oil, complemented by *"hybrid authoritarianism"* that has deepened during the Maduro government. This authoritarianism has resulted, for example, in censorship of the media, imprisonment of opposition leaders, and the holding of formal but illegitimate electoral processes. However, Maduro has not counted on the voluminous oil rents that his predecessor had, due to a drastic reduction of international oil prices. Therefore, in the face of significant reduction of oil rents for clientelist purposes and for the weakening of the opposition, Maduro has increasingly resorted to repression and coercion as a mechanism of domestic social and political control (Mejía, 2018).

The "Independent international fact-finding mission on the Bolivarian Republic of Venezuela" (IIFFMBRV) identifies the worst deterioration of democratic institutions in Venezuela between December 2015 and December 2016, *"after the opposition won a majority of seats in the National Assembly"* (Human Rights Council, 2020, p. 5). However, before the new National Assembly was installed in January 2016, the government nominated and appointed 13 justices and 21 substitutes at the Supreme Court of Justice, securing loyalty of the high court; therefore, *"the Supreme Court of Justice has continuously struck down laws that the legislature attempted to pass"* (Human Rights Council, 2020, p. 3). Finally, in September of that year, *"the Supreme Court held that all National Assembly legislation was null and void"* (Human Rights Council, 2020, p. 3), after ruling that the Assembly didn't comply with an order that prohibited it from swearing in the legislators of the state of Amazonas. This situation generated an institutional confrontation that has accentuated: Nicolás Maduro has not been recognized as legitimate President by most countries, while interim President Juan Guaidó has not been recognized as legitimate by the armed forces of Venezuela.

Then, in 2017 Maduro restricted the participation of opposition leaders in national elections, which caused that, among other reasons, his regime was characterized by the international community as *"dictatorial, autocratic, and repressive"* (López Maya, 2018, p. 47). Due to its institutional deterioration, generalized impunity, and the arbitrary and excessive use of force, during Maduro's administration international entities such as Amnesty International have registered cases of (i) systematic violation of freedom of expression, (ii) massive violation of freedom of assembly, (iii) arbitrary arrest and detention, (iv) excessive use of force, (v) torture, (vi) attacks on human rights defenders, (vii) high levels of impunity in the justice system, (viii) violation of the right to food, (ix) violation of the right to health and (x) violation of sexual and reproductive rights (Amnesty International, 2018).In fact, the Office of the United Nations High Commissioner for Human Rights has urged *"the Government of Venezuela to immediately adopt specific measures to stop and remedy the serious violations of economic, social, civil, political and cultural rights that have been documented in the country"* (Office of the United Nations High Commissioner for Human Rights, 2019). These violations are closely related to corruption: as the IIFFMBRV has pointed out, in Venezuela, corruption is reinforced in a perverse circle with the systematic violation of human rights (Human Rights Council, 2020).

It is striking that Venezuela's Corruption Perception Index in 2019 was even worse than that of North Korea, which is perhaps the most repressive and opaque dictatorial regime today. Venezuela ranks 173 in the corruption perception index out of 180 countries, the worst in Latin America, and its Human Development Index is similar to that of Zimbabwe, Azerbaijan and countries in Central Asia (Mungiu-Pippidi, 2017). In this sense, the economic effects of corruption and institutional deterioration have not necessarily been the most relevant, even though the International Monetary Fund registered an inflation rate of 200,000% in 2019. Without a doubt, one of the most serious effects has been humanitarian in terms of deteriorating health, malnutrition and lack of food, and unprecedented levels of migration abroad. Thus, for example: in 2016 the infant mortality rate increased between 30% and 40%, compared to 2008 (Garcia, Correa, & Rousset, 2019), in 2019 doctors warned that Venezuela registered the largest increase in the incidence of malaria in the world with between 600,000 to one million cases (El País, 2019), and over 4 million refugees left the country between 2014 and 2019, which also has no antecedents in the region (UNHCR, 2019).

Precisely due to humanitarian effects such as the situation of violation of human rights that has worsened since 2014 (Human Rights Council, 2020), the Maduro regime cannot be defined solely as an extension of Chavism but as characterized by exceptional use of force and by a strict relationship between corruption and systematic violation of human rights. These elements have established a kleptocratic regime that has substantially reconfiguring the rule of law and the democratic system through a complex structure of macro-corruption and institutional co-optation, which is analyzed in the following chapters.

III. The Super Network

As noted in the introduction, the model analyzed herein is referred to as a "super network" because it exceeds by more than two orders of magnitude the size of networks previously defined by Salcedo-Albarán & Garay-Salamanca (2016) as macro networks, which is precisely the same criterion applied to the concept of macro-corruption (Garay Salamanca, Salcedo-Albarán, & Macías, 2018d). This super network reflects the massive and systematic co-optation of public institutions in the Venezuelan State, to favor illicit interests of powerful nodes/agents.

The nodes/agents and their interactions identified in the super network of macro-corruption and institutional co-optation of Venezuela were classified according to categories used in previous models of illicit networks, as well as other categories defined during the process of systematization.With the Interactions Database (IdB), 5,748 nodes/agents were identified, including natural and legal persons[2], who established 17,493 interactions (Table 1), illustrated in Figure 1. Although the exact number of nodes/agents and interactions changes as additional information is systematized, the large numbers allow us to understand the magnitude of this super network of corruption.

As shown in Table 1, the most statistically relevant categories of interactions are: (i) those describing appointments to positions, (ii) those reporting on the role of people appointed to public and private positions, and (iii) those describing acts of corruption. Although the interaction category of corruption is analyzed in detail in the following sections, the first two categories about appointments to public positions are not alien to the dynamics of corruption; in fact, clientelism, understood as the appointment of public officials in exchange for favors and partisan purposes, is one of the

---

[2] In this case, the category of legal entities includes public entities involved or affected by the macro-corruption structure.

main mechanisms to consolidate the co-option of institutions of the Venezuelan State.

In other words, the process of massive co-optation in Venezuela is not necessarily carried out through traditional bribery, but rather through control and manipulation of instances of public decision to (i) manage and allocate large amounts public resources in favor of specific agents, and (ii) conduct political processes under clientelist or patrimonial criteria. This has mainly happened by appointing family members and officials who support government interests, not only at the executive branch but across all sectors and levels of public administration, including judicial instances and parastatal companies.

In this regard, it is important to point out that "government interests" not only refer to public policies promoted by the executive branch; in the case of Venezuela, "government interests" also implies control of the legislative and judicial branches, with decisions characterized by discretion, opacity, impunity, concentration of power and, therefore, prone to massive co-optation and corruption. In this sense, patrimonialism, clientelism and nepotism are the main mechanisms to sustain macro-corruption and institutional co-optation reproduced in the super network.

In the super network of macro-corruption and co-optation in Venezuela there are more than 100 interactions that explicitly describe human rights violations. Although statistically irrelevant in the context of the super network, these interactions are significant because in other cases of macro-corruption no interactions of this type have been recorded; in fact, in a network of macro-corruption and institutional co-optation as extensive, complex, and transnational as *Lava Jato*, no direct interactions have been identified that describe human rights violations.

The nodes/agents of the super network were classified into two main categories, namely: natural persons or individuals (66%) and organizations, corporations, or entities – that is, legal persons (31%). Regarding the high number of legal entities, it is mainly due to the illegal money laundering schemes that sustain the macro-corruption processes observed in this super network. As discussed in the following sections, due to the large amount of illegally appropriated public resources, the agents involved usually require transnational money laundering structures to transfer and "legitimize" those resources. These money laundering structures are carried out through façade or "briefcase" companies established to simulate contracts and payments, to transfer illegal assets through bank accounts around the world.

Table 1. Distribution of categories of interactions in the super network of macro-corruption and institutional co-optation in Venezuela.

Interaction type	Quantity	%
Positions taken	6660	38.1
Designated persons	6187	35.4
Corruption facts	1408	8.0
Other	678	3.9
Business friends	588	3.4
Related news	526	3.0
Companies created	500	2.9
Family	366	2.1
International sanctions	344	2.0
Human Rights Violations	118	0.7
Study friends	85	0.5
Military friends	10	0.1
Irregular decisions	8	0.0
Undefined	5	0.0
Contract	4	0.0
Enemies	4	0.0
Related news - CLAP	1	0.0
Total	**17493**	**100**

Direct Interactions, Resource Flows and Network's Resilience

Table 2 shows the group of 10 nodes/agents that establish the highest proportion of direct interactions in the super network, which altogether accounts for 17.40% of the total. This set, represented by the nodes/agents closest to the core in Figure 2, is led by Nicolás Maduro, who concentrates 3.60% of all direct interactions in the super network and acts as the structure's *hub*, therefore is located at the core of the graph. As discussed in the previous section, after inheriting the presidency on an interim basis in 2013, following the death of Chávez, Nicolás Maduro has not only continued with the political agenda of his predecessor but, given the lack of public resources that Chávez had at his disposal, he has exercised violent repression to counteract any initiative of political and social opposition, and thus to impose a domestic agenda mediated by massive corruption, violation of human rights and State terrorism.

Table 2. Ten nodes/agents with the highest direct centrality indicator. Super network of macro-corruption and institutional co-optation in Venezuela.

Node/agent	% Direct Centrality
Nicolás Maduro Moros	3.601441
José David Cabello Rondón	2.926885
Servicio Nacional Integrado de Administración Aduanera y Tributaria (SENIAT)	2.280912
Tareck Zaidan El Aissami Maddah	1.880752
Néstor Luis Reverol Torres	1.683531
Carlos Alberto Osorio Zambrano	1.514892
Ministerio de Relaciones Exteriores	1.409135
Carlos Erik Malpica Flores	1.111873
Elías José Jaua Milano	0.994684

Although the Organization of American States and several countries have not recognized Maduro as the legitimate president of Venezuela since October 2019, the domestic loyalty of the Military Forces has allowed Maduro to exercise repression complemented by a clientelist network that extends throughout the public administration and that guarantees the permanence of the regime. This, however, does not imply that the loyalty of the Venezuelan Military Forces is necessarily explained only by ideological coincidence, but also possibly by clientelism and economic and political favors that certain powerful militaries have received through appointments to key decision-making positions. The exacerbated clientelism that Maduro has promoted is reflected in that he acts as an active node/agent or issuer in 75% of the direct interactions that he establishes; in turn, most of the interactions in which Maduro participates are classified as "designated persons", meaning that he directly or indirectly influences their appointment as public officials.

Considering the high degree of concentration of power in the Venezuelan Executive Branch, which coincides with the "presidential" tradition in Latin America, Nicolás Maduro occupies the highest decision-making position in the country, without checks and balances or accountability; for this reason, it is striking the relatively high number of direct interactions that this node/agent registers in the super network. As the president, it could be expected that Maduro interacts across the super network through a small close circle of advisers in charge of managing instructions and spreading information in the chain of command; however, it is observed that he directly interacts with several nodes/agents, even with peripherals. This coincides with the findings that in Venezuela *"the President at times circumvented the established chains of command to issue orders directly to mid-level members"* of the State security entities (Human Rights Council, 2020, p. 405), which is reflected in the high indicator of direct centrality that he registers in the super network.

On the other hand, José David Cabello Rondón, brother of Diosdado Cabello Rondón, registers the second highest proportion of direct interactions (2.93%) in the super network. Considering the domestic and international relevance of Diosdado Cabello it would be expected that he plays a relevant role in the articulation of the super network. To this effect, it calls the attention that Diosdado Cabello does not appears among the 10 nodes/agents with the highest direct centrality indicator, but José David Cabello, as the second one.

The high relevance of José David Cabello as an articulator of the super network can be understood when considering his positions in the Venezuelan public administration: minister of infrastructure since 2006, and then director of the National Integrated Service for the Administration of Customs Duties and Taxes (SENIAT) since February 2008. In this sense, his current position as director of the SENIAT explains why this entity appears as the third node/agent with the highest proportion of direct interactions in the super network, which allows inferring that the entity has been manipulated and used for corruption and other illicit purposes.

Furthermore, as can be seen in Table 3, Nicolás Maduro also registers the highest indicator of intervention capacity, or betweenness. This means that Maduro is not only the hub of the super network, with the highest indicator of direct centrality, but he is also the structural bridge, with the highest indicator of betweenness. In other words, Maduro simultaneously concentrates the highest percentage of direct interactions and the greatest capacity to intervene in the flows – or indirect routes– of the super network.

A similar role as key articulator of the super network can be observed in the case of José David Cabello Rondón who, as well as registering the second highest indicator of direct centrality, also has the second highest indicator of betweenness, or capacity for intervention. Since it can be inferred that these two nodes/agents play a relevant articulating role, they can also be interpreted as potentially bearing the greatest responsibility of the macro-corruption, the institutional cooptation, and the human rights violation observed in the super network.

Tareck Zaidan El Aissami Maddah registers the third highest indicator of betweenness (6.70%) and, therefore, the third highest capacity to intervene in the geodesic routes of the network. This node/agent was elected in 2005 as a deputy to the National Assembly for the United Socialist Party of Venezuela (PSUV), appointed in 2008 Minister of Internal Affairs by Hugo Chávez, and who in 2020 served as Minister of Industry and National Production of Venezuela.

Table 3. Ten nodes/agents with the highest betweenness indicator. Super network of macro-corruption and institutional co-optation in Venezuela.

Node/agent	% Betweenness
Nicolás Maduro Moros	18.502137
José David Cabello Rondón	8.303097
Tareck Zaidan El Aissami Maddah	6.693351
Hugo Rafael Chávez Frías	4.196995
Néstor Luis Reverol Torres	3.567828
Carlos Erik Malpica Flores	2.677207
Rafael Darío Ramírez Carreño	2.512958
Diosdado Cabello Rondón	2.422177
Carlos Alberto Osorio Zambrano	2.105083
Elías José Jaua Milano	1.549993

Since 2019, Tareck Zaidan El Aissami Maddah is considered by the United States border authorities as one of the 10 most wanted international drug trafficking fugitives, after noting that he has used his position of power to facilitate the trafficking of *"shipments of over 1,000 kilograms that left Venezuela on multiple occasions, including those whose final destination was Mexico and the United States"* (BBC News, 2019).

That said, it is striking that Hugo Chávez shows up as the fourth node/agent with the highest betweenness indicator, even though he is not part of the group of 10 nodes/agents with the highest direct centrality indicator. Of course, Chávez did not established direct appointments interactions since his death in 2014, which explains his low direct centrality indicator; however, as he was president of Venezuela, promoting and defending his policies, it is expected that flows of resources established during his military and political career continue to support a super network that currently still operates based on his political and administrative actions. For this reason, Chávez shows up as one of the nodes/agents close to the core in Figure 3, which illustrates the super network in terms of the betweenness indicator.

In total, the set of 10 nodes/agents presented in Table 3 concentrates 52.5% out of the betweenness indicator, that is, the total resource flows of the structure. The fact that 0.6% of nodes/agents intervene in more than half of the resource flows of the super network, implies a high concentration of decision power around these few nodes/agents. Therefore, a relatively low level of resilience can be inferred since it would be necessary to isolate less than 1% of nodes/agents to intervene and modify the structural operation of more than half of the resource flows of the structure.

Basic Corruption Subnetwork

To analyze the subnetwork specifically aimed at committing acts of corruption, those interactions related to bribery management, clientelism and nepotism were selected and analyzed. The result of this analysis is the subnetwork illustrated in Figure 4, with Nicolás Maduro Moros as structural bridge, followed by Raúl Antonio de la Santísima Trinidad, who jointly intervene in 16% of the geodesic routes of the sub-structure. Although Nicolás Maduro Moros is a structural bridge for both the corruption subnetwork and the super network, Raúl Antonio de la Santísima Trinidad Gorrín is only relevant in the case of the corruption subnetwork.

According to the U.S. Immigration and Customs Enforcement (ICE) agency, Gorrín took advantage of his activities as a lawyer and businessman to commit acts of corruption and money laundering; specifically, according to the indictment, *"paid millions of dollars in bribes to two high-level Venezuelan officials to secure the rights to conduct foreign currency exchange transactions at favorable rates (…). In addition to wiring money to bribe the officials, he allegedly purchased and paid expenses for them related to private jets, yachts, homes, champion horses, high-end watches, and a fashion line (…). In addition to transferring money to pay bribes to officers, he allegedly also purchased and paid for these officers' expenses related to private jets, yachts, fine horses, fine watches, and a fashion line (...) through multiple shell companies (and) partnered with other subjects to acquire Banco Peravia, a bank in the Dominican Republic, to launder the bribes paid to Venezuelan officials"* (US Immigration and Customs Enforcement, 2020).

In this subnetwork, the 8 nodes/agents with the highest indicator of betweenness intervene in 52% out of the resource flows; in other words, 0.85% of nodes/agents (8 out of 934) intervene in more than half of the subnetwork's geodesic routes. Based on the foregoing, it can be inferred that this subnetwork specifically focused on acts of corruption shows a relatively low level of resiliency, like the super network. Table 4 shows the set of nodes/agents that intervene in more than half of the flows in this subnetwork.

Table 4. Group of 8 nodes/agents with the highest betweenness indicator in the "basic corruption" subnetwork.
Super network of macro-corruption and institutional co-optation in Venezuela.

Node/agent - Basic corruption	Betweenness %
Nicolás Maduro Moros	8.16
Raúl Antonio De la Santísima Trinidad Gorrín Belisario	8.15
Hugo Armando Carvajal Barrios	6.52
Diosdado Cabello Rondón	6.49
Rafael Darío Ramírez Carreño	6.23
Alejandro Leopoldo Betancourt López	5.87
Petróleos de Venezuela, S.A. (PDVSA)	5.59
Roberto Enrique Rincón Fernández	5.08

Human Rights Violations Subnetwork

As previously noted, multilateral organizations and international entities have documented a systematic violation of human rights in Venezuela (Amnesty International, 2018; UNHCR, 2019; Human Rights Watch, 2017; Human Rights Council, 2020). Bearing this in mind, the subnetwork of human rights violations was also considered in this analysis and visualized in Figures 5 and 6.

In this subnetwork Nicolás Maduro is also identified as the node/agent with the highest indicator of betweenness and, therefore, with greater capacity to intervene in the flows of resources specifically aimed at committing human rights violations. Additionally, as the second node/agent closest to the core, Figure 6 shows the Bolivarian National Intelligence Service (SEBIN), an entity that has been used by the government to commonly exercise coercion through *"severe beatings, (...) electric shocks, suffocation, and other techniques"* of torture (Human Rights Watch, 2017).

The fact that the SEBIN shows up as the second structural bridge that articulates the subnetwork of human rights violations in Venezuela coincides with reports by the United Nations IIFFMBRV, according to which SEBIN agents *"threatened to rape men, women and their families"* during an interrogation at the Helicoide penitentiary (Human Rights Council, 2020, p. 378), while in another case SEBIN agents *"participated in the extrajudicial executions of five young people"* (Human Rights Council, 2020, p. 236). In fact, *"former SEBIN Director Christopher Figuera told the Mission that, upon taking up his position at the end of October 2018, he discovered what he described as 'a culture of torture' within SEBIN, which pre-dated his appointment"* (Human Rights Council, 2020, p. 384). As discussed in the final chapter of the book, the events committed in the context of SEBIN activities should be the object of special attention to reconstruct the memory of human rights violations committed within and by this entity.

Figure 7 illustrates the structure that articulates the subnetworks of corruption and human rights violations, made up of 997 nodes/agents that establish 1,969 interactions altogether. Although the subnetwork shown in Figure 7 is comprised mostly of nodes/agents involved only in the corruption subnetwork, there is a set of nodes/agents with high betweenness indicator who participate simultaneously in both subnetworks. The difference in the betweenness indicators is evidenced by comparing Tables 4 and 5.

Table 5. Group of 8 nodes/agents with the highest betweenness indicator in the subnetwork of "basic corruption" and "human rights violations". Super network of macro-corruption and institutional co-optation in Venezuela.

Node/agent	Betweenness (%)
Nicolás Maduro Moros	10.60
Raúl Antonio De la Santísima Trinidad Gorrín Belisario	9.31
Alejandro Leopoldo Betancourt López	6.44
Petróleos de Venezuela, S.A. (PDVSA)	6.31
Diosdado Cabello Rondón	5.85
Rafael Darío Ramírez Carreño	5.09
Hugo Armando Carvajal Barrios	5.04
Roberto Enrique Rincón Fernández	3.92

Macro-corruption Subnetwork in the Food Sector

In 2019, Venezuela had the fourth worst food crisis in the world, surpassed only by Yemen, the Democratic Republic of the Congo and Afghanistan, with 32% of the population (9.3 million people) in a situation of food insecurity and in need of emergency assistance. In fact, in Venezuela *"60% are in a situation of marginal insecurity"* (Global Networks Against Food Crisis & Food Security Information Network, 2020, p. 185).

Bearing this in mind, the interactions that specifically inform about macro-corruption in the food sector were selected, mainly related to contracts to acquire and distribute food under government assistance programs. The result is a subnetwork made up of 503 nodes/agents that established 881 interactions, illustrated in Figure 8.

In this subnetwork, Carlos Alberto Osorio Zambrano, ex-military and *Chavista* leader, is registered as the structural bridge with the highest betweenness indicator, intervening in 33.03% out of the geodesic routes of the subnetwork. Osorio Zambrano has served in various positions as Minister of Transport and Minister in the President's Office. However, in the articulation of the subnetwork related to macro-corruption in the food sector, his most relevant roles have been as vice president for food security and sovereignty, and serving two times as minister of The Ministry of Popular Power for the Food. In 2017, Osorio Zambrano was included in a list of individuals sanctioned by the United States Department of the Treasury for acts to *"affect electoral processes, censor the media, or [for] corruption in food programs administered by the government."* (US Department of the Treasury, 2017).

Osorio Zambrano is not only relevant in the subnetwork related to macro-corruption in the food sector but also in the super network, with an immediate social structure of 177 nodes/agents and an influence network within two degrees of separation that reaches 842 nodes/agents. This high influencing capacity is striking when compared, for example, with that of Diosdado Cabello Rondón, whose immediate social network consists of 182 nodes/agents and his influence network within two degrees of separation reaches 573 nodes/agents.

As observed in Table 6, the second node/agent with the highest betweenness indicator in the subnetwork related to macro-corruption in the food sector is Nicolás Maduro, which means that Osorio Zambrano and Maduro intervene jointly in more than half of the subnetwork's geodesic routes (62.43%). This high concentration in the intervention capacity allows inferring a low level of resilience of the subnetwork, since the actions of only two nodes/agents affect almost two thirds of the geodesic routes and resource flows in the subnetwork.

Table 6. Ten nodes/agents with the highest betweenness indicator in the macro-corruption subnetwork in the food sector of Venezuela.
Super network of macro-corruption and institutional co-optation in Venezuela.

Node/agent	Betweenness (%)
Carlos Alberto Osorio Zambrano	33.03
Nicolás Maduro Moros	29.40
Elías José Jaua Milano	6.10
Hugo Rafael Chávez Frías	4.58
Rodolfo Clemente Marco Torres	4.21
Ramon Rafael Campos Cabello	3.87
Wilmar Alfredo Castro Soteldo	2.33
Tibisay Yanette Lenín Castro	2.15
Alba Patróleos de El Salvador (Albapes)	1.63

Macro-corruption Subnetwork
in the Oil Sector

As noted at the beginning of the book, the oil sector is one of the main scenarios for macro-corruption and institutional co-option in Venezuela. As a result of the high oil revenues that the Venezuelan State received especially during the first decade of this century, this sector has been scenario of the main corruption cases in the country. In fact, Transparencia Venezuela has identified 28 cases of corruption in the management of oil revenues that are carried out in international jurisdictions, compromising important public resources that amount to over USD$25 billion (Transparencia Venezuela, 2019).

Considering the above, a subnetwork was modeled and analyzed by selecting those interactions that specifically report on macro-corruption processes in the public administration and management of oil revenues; that is, bribes and diversion of resources throughout the institutional framework of companies and entities of the Venezuelan oil sector. As a result, the subnetwork related to macro-corruption in the oil sector illustrated in Figure 9 is made up of 309 nodes/agents that establish 514 interactions.

Table 7 shows how Nicolás Maduro appears as the structural bridge of the subnetwork with a betweenness indicator of 26.97%, that is, intervening in more than a quarter of the total geodesic routes and flows of the subnetwork. With the second largest indicator of betweenness appears the Petróleos de Venezuela Company, PDVSA, with an indicator of 13.80%. Therefore, it is inferred that Nicolás Maduro intervenes in more than 40% of geodesic routes of the macro-corruption subnetwork at the Venezuelan oil sector, especially through the institutional cooptation and manipulation of PDVSA. In fact, the relevance of Nicolás Maduro coopting this entity is also reflected by the direct centrality indicator (Table 8) since the company appears as a *hub* of the subnetwork with an indicator of 13.3%, and Nicolás Maduro as the node/agent with the second highest concentration of direct interactions, with 6.4%.

Table 7. Ten nodes/agents with the highest betweenness indicator in the "Macro-corruption Subnetwork in the Oil Sector".
Super network of macro-corruption and institutional co-optation in Venezuela.

Node/agent	Betweenness (%)
Nicolás Maduro Moros	26.96
Petróleos de Venezuela S.A. (PDVSA)	13.80
Hugo Rafael Chávez Frías	10.07
Rafael Darío Ramírez Carreño	8.61
Manuel Salvador Quevedo Fernandez	7.61
Alba Petróleos de El Salvador (Albapes)	4.95
Petrosur S.A.	4.46
José Ramón Blanco Balín	4.39
Alejandro Leopoldo Betancourt López	3.03
Francisco Antonio Convit Guruceaga	2.30

Table 8. Ten nodes/agents with the highest direct centrality indicator in the "Macro-corruption Subnetwork in the Oil Sector".
Super network of macro-corruption and institutional co-optation in Venezuela.

Node/agent	Direct Centrality (%)
Petróleos de Venezuela S.A. (PDVSA)	13.3
Nicolás Maduro Moros	6.4
Francisco Morillo	4.3
Alba Petróleos de El Salvador (Albapes)	3.1
CITGO Petroleum Corporation	2.5
Rafael Darío Ramírez Carreño	2.2
Manuel Salvador Quevedo Fernandez	1.9
Hugo Rafael Chávez Frías	1.6
Nervis Gerardo Villalobos Cárdenas	1.5
Francisco Antonio Convit Guruceaga	1.4

Geodesic routes

The previous analysis reveals the importance not only of understanding the characteristics and dynamics of the super network, but also of the subnetworks in which the relevant role of specific nodes/agents and their forms of interaction are evidenced. In fact, after understanding their relevant role, it is also important to specify how the flows of resources develop among the most relevant nodes/agents. In this sense, the following chapter is dedicated to analyze the geodesic routes and the resource flows established between some of the most important nodes/agents in the super network, paying special attention to the number of geodesic routes that connect them. As will be discussed, in some cases, numerous geodesic routes that indirectly connect two nodes/agents are identified, which drastically increases the complexity of subnetworks such as those dedicated to money laundering.

Figure 1. Super network of macro-corruption and institutional co-optation in Venezuela.

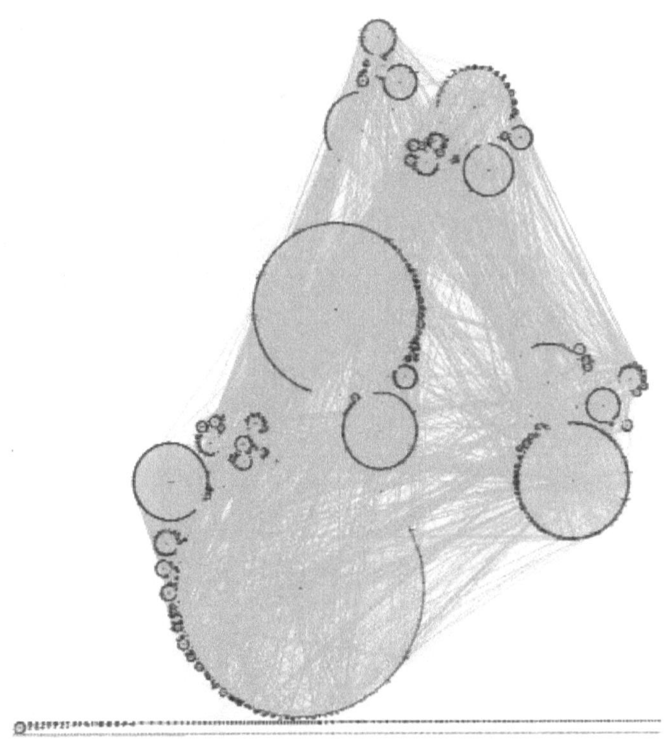

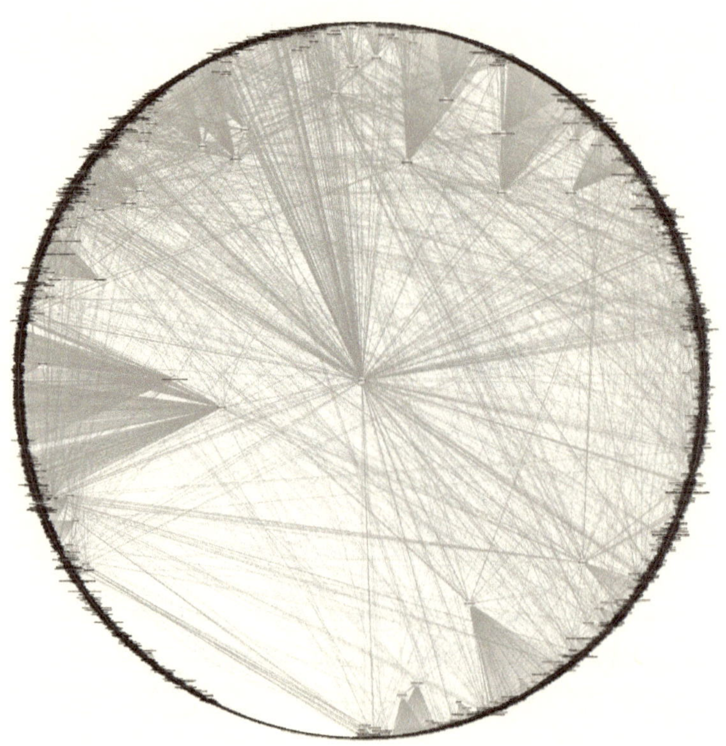

Figure 2. Super network of macro-corruption and institutional co-optation in Venezuela.
The size and location of nodes/agents represent the direct centrality indicator.

Figure 3. Super network of macro-corruption and co-optation in Venezuela. The size and location of nodes/agents represent the betweenness indicator.

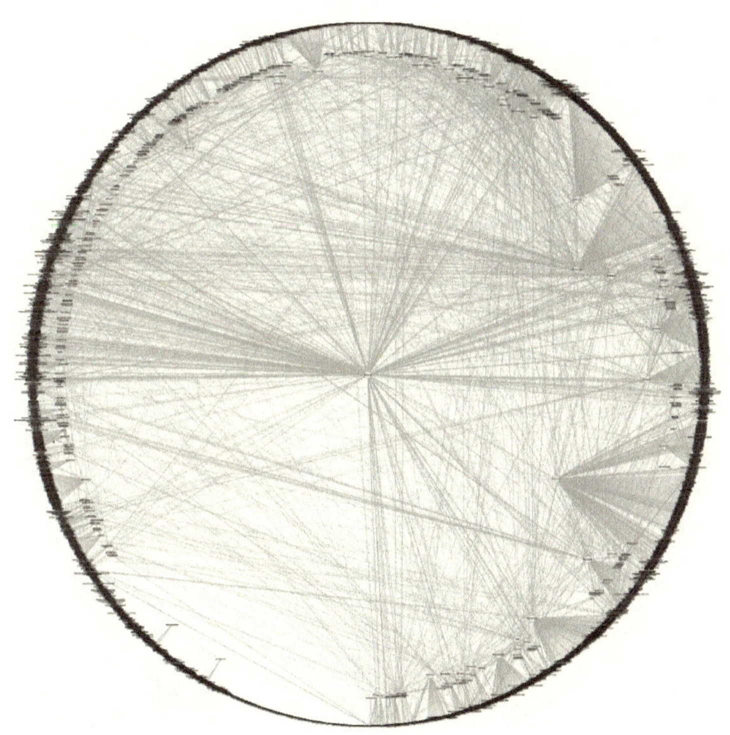

Figure 4. Subnetwork of "basic corruption" (dark lines) in the super network of macro-corruption and institutional co-optation in Venezuela.
The size and location of nodes/agents represent the capacity to intervene in the network's geodesic routes (betweenness indicator).

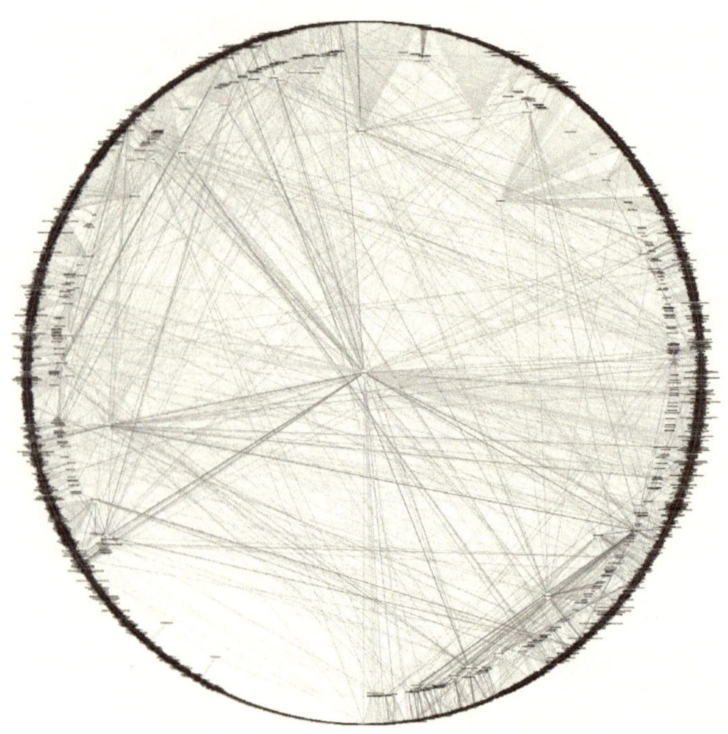

Figure 5. Subnetwork of "human rights violations" extracted from the super network of macro-corruption and institutional co-optation in Venezuela. The size of the nodes/agents represents the capacity to intervene in the network's geodesic routes (betweenness indicator). Thicker lines represent a higher frequency of interactions.

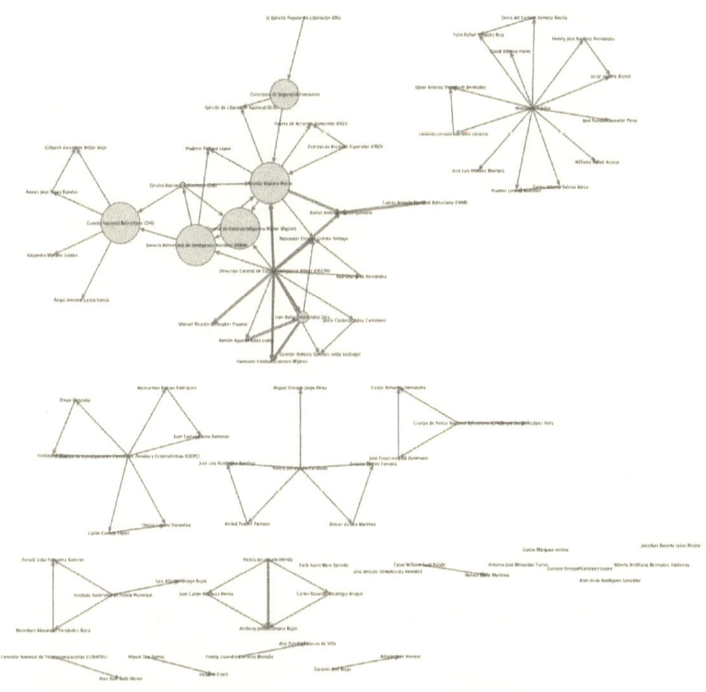

Figure 6. Subnetwork of "human rights violations" extracted from the super network of macro-corruption and institutional co-optation in Venezuela. The size and location of nodes/agents (higher in the core) represent the capacity to intervene in the network's geodesic routes (betweenness indicator).

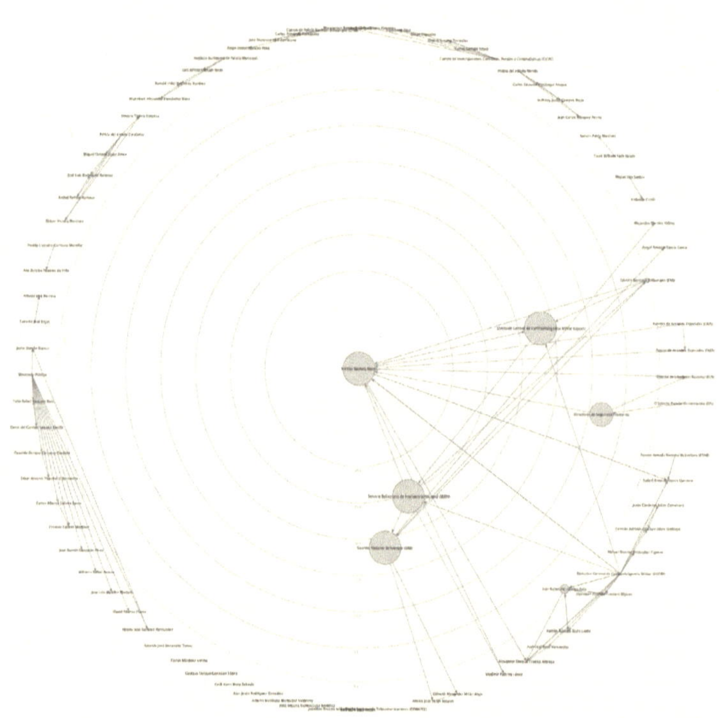

Figure 7. Subnetwork of "basic corruption" and "human rights violation" combined, extracted from the super network of macro-corruption and institutional co-optation in Venezuela.
The size and location of the nodes/agents (higher in the core) represent the capacity to intervene in the network's geodesic routes (betweenness indicator).

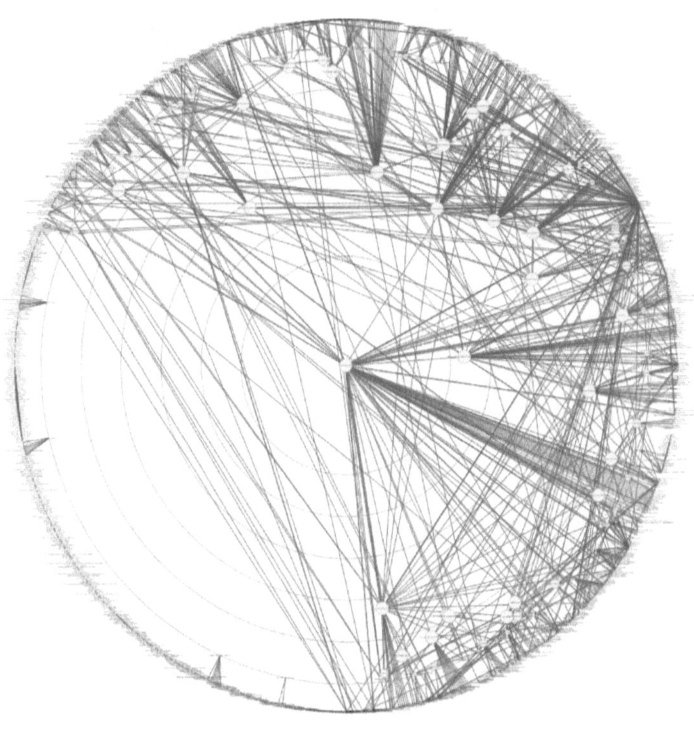

Figure 8. Venezuela's "macro-corruption in the food sector" subnetwork. The size of the nodes/agents represents the capacity to intervene in the network's geodesic routes (betweenness indicator).

Figure 9. Venezuela's "macro-corruption in the oil sector" subnetwork. The size of the nodes/agents represents the capacity to intervene in the network's geodesic routes (betweenness indicator).

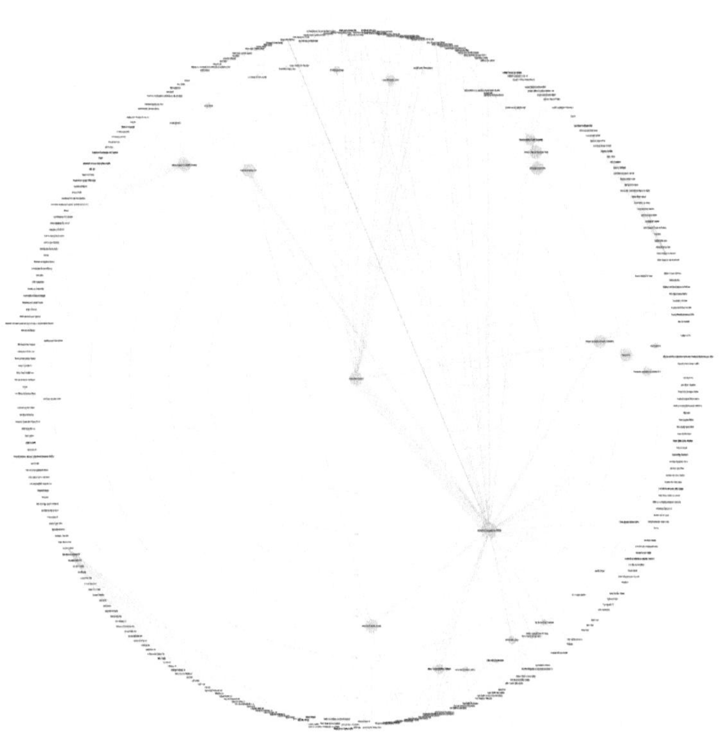

IV. The Routes of Nepotism and Kleptocracy

As pointed out in the previous chapter, the betweenness indicator informs about the capacity of a node/agent to intervene in the network's geodesic routes. This is important because in social networks, including illicit ones, resources flow through geodesic routes. For example, resources such as money or information can be transmitted directly from a node/agent A to a node/agent B, and then from B to other nodes/agents C, D, and E, even without A having originally intended to transmit resources to *C, D,* and *E.* In fact, even ignoring the existence or the interests of nodes/agents *C, D,* or *E,* node/agent *A* can transmit resources indirectly to them, thanks to the action of a node/agent *B,* as illustrated in Figure 10.

Figure 10. Indirect transmission of resources from agents A to C, D, and E, through agent B.

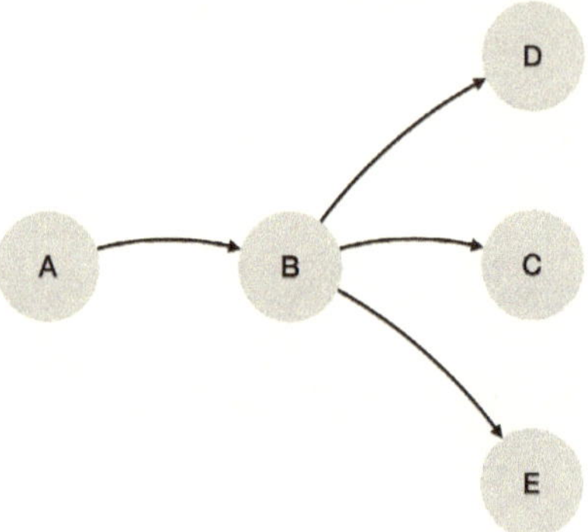

Assuming that the resources are transmitted sequentially between *A, B, C, D,* and *E,* as in Figure 11, then there is a potential geodesic route made up of 5 nodes/agents that indirectly connect the nodes/agents A and E.

Figure 11. Geodesic route from node/agent A to node/agent E.

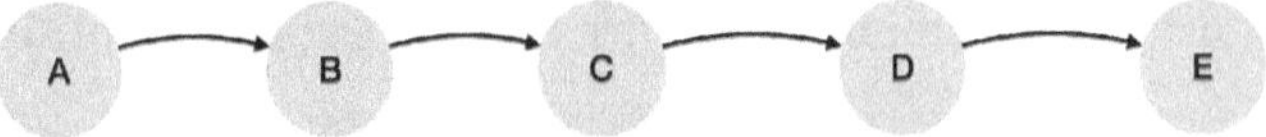

Accordingly, it is crucial not only to analyze the direct interactions that are established in a network, but also the geodesic routes through which resources flow; this is why in the previous chapter the betweenness indicator was calculated and analyzed, to understand the capacity of some nodes/agents to intervene in geodesic routes regardless of their number of direct interactions. However, the analysis of geodesic routes that indirectly connect two nodes/agents is especially important when analyzing illicit schemes such as money laundering, which are established to hide the true origin, destination, and direct and indirect beneficiaries of illicit money.

The success of a money laundering scheme is expected to be related to the number of nodes/agents that make up its geodesic routes; that is, the more extensive and the more nodes/agents a money laundering route includes, *ceteris paribus*, the more difficult it is for the authorities to identify it and prosecute those agents involved. For example, if node/agent A pays a bribe directly to node/agent E, then the authorities will identify this payment more easily than if the money first flows through B, C, and D.

Considering the importance of understanding the resource flows within a network as complex as that observed in Venezuela, the routes that connect some relevant nodes/agents (Table 9) with Nicolás Maduro were calculated and analyzed. By identifying the number of geodesic routes between each pair of nodes/agents, it is possible to infer the greater or lesser proportion of resources that flowed directly and indirectly between them. This calculation was developed with algorithms traditionally used in bioinformatics to analyze the transmission of signals and the effects of transformations through extensive networks (Vera-Licona, Bonnet, Barillot, & Zinovyev, 2013).

In the first column of Table 9 the source node/agent is identified, in the second column, the number of nodes/agents that appears in the second place of the geodesic routes that connect the source agent with Nicolás Maduro is indicated, and the third column specifies the number of geodesic routes connecting the source node/agent with Nicolás Maduro as target or arrival agent.

Table 9. Geodesic routes that indirectly connect some relevant nodes/ agents with Nicolás Maduro, who is the hub and structural bridge of the super network.

Outbound node/agent	Number of immediate nodes/agents, or second nodes/agents in the geodesic route	Number of routes identified with Nicolás Maduro (target or arrival node/agent)
José David Cabello Rondón	12	278,750
Nervis Gerardo Villalobos Cárdenas	17	48,360
Carlos Alberto Osorio	9	40,613
Diosdado Cabello Rondón	33	27,693
Haiman El Troudi Douwara	5	11,333
Samark José López	5	5,478
Alex Naim Saab Morán	35	2,705

There are 2,705 geodesic routes indirectly connecting Alex Naim Saab Morán with Nicolás Maduro, in which 35 nodes/agents occupy the second position of the routes; that is, Alex Naim Saab Morán interacts with 35 nodes/agents immediately to establish the 2,705 geodesic routes that connect him to Nicolás Maduro. However, this does not mean that the 2,705 routes originate uniformly from the 35 nodes/

agents, since more geodesic routes emerge from some of them; this means that some second/intermediary agents facilitate the establishment of more routes.

The proportion of 35 nodes/agents with whom Alex Naim Saab Morán interacts directly to establish the 2,705 geodesic routes with Nicolás Maduro contrasts with the proportion observed in the case of José David Cabello Rondón, who graduated from the military academy with his brother Diosdado Cabello, and who interacts directly with 12 nodes/agents to establish 278,750 geodesic routes with Nicolás Maduro.

When comparing Alex Naim Saab Morán with José David Cabello Rondón, it is found that Saab Morán interacts directly with more nodes/agents to establish fewer geodesic routes, while Cabello Rondón interacts directly with fewer nodes/agents to establish more geodesic routes. In this sense, some nodes/agents act more stealthily in the network, by establishing and exposing themselves to few direct interactions but establishing numerous geodesic routes, while other nodes/agents that act less stealthy exposed themselves to many direct interactions to form proportionally fewer geodesic routes. In fact, the ratio between the number of geodesic routes and the number of direct interactions, parameterized by the higher ratio between the second intermediary nodes/agents, can be expressed in terms of a stealthy indicator, such as the one shown in Tables 10 and 11.

Table 10. Proportion of direct interactions and geodesic routes for some relevant nodes/agents of the super network.

Outbound node/agent	Number of immediate nodes/agents, or second nodes/agents in the geodesic route	Number of routes identified with Nicolás Maduro (arrival or target node/agent)	Proportion
José David Cabello Rondón	12	278,750	23,229.17
Nervis Gerardo Villalobos Cárdenas	17	48,360	2,844.71
Carlos Alberto Osorio	9	40,613	4,512.56
Diosdado Cabello Rondón	33	27,693	839.18
Haiman El Troudi Douwara	5	11,333	2,266.60
Samark José	5	5,478	1,095.60
Alex Nain Saab Morán	35	2,705	77.29

Table 11. Stealth indicator for some relevant nodes/agents of the super network.

Node/agent	Stealth Indicator
José David Cabello Rondón	1.0000
Carlos Alberto Osorio	0.1222
Haiman El Troudi Douwara	0.1937
Samark José	0.0361
Diosdado Cabello Rondón	0.0975
Nervis Gerardo Villalobos Cárdenas	0.0471
Alex Naim Saab Morán	0.0033

The stealth indicator reflects the ability of some nodes/agents to strategically manage their direct and immediate interactions, reducing their exposure by establishing few direct interactions that are highly useful to maximize the number of geodesic-indirect routes. In this sense, a node/agent such as José David Cabello Rondón is highly stealthy – the highest among the second nodes/ intermediary agents considered in Table 10 –, parameterized with a value equal to 1. This stealthy feature requires the strategic selection of their direct interactions because, as noted, not all network nodes/agents have the same capacity to facilitate the flow of resources in the network, from and to Nicolás Maduro. Similarly, it can be inferred that a node/agent such as Alex Naim Saab Morán is less *stealthy* – with a parameterized value of 0.0033 –, establishing a high number of direct interactions to achieve a relatively lower flow of resources with Nicolás Maduro. In fact, this relatively lower level of stealthy contribute to explain why Alex Naim Saab Morán was targeted by US authorities and then captured by the Cape Verdean authorities in June 2020 under the US judicial solicitude of extradition (Delgado, 2020).

The strategic selection of the immediate nodes/agents in the establishment of the geodesic routes is reflected in Table 12, which reports on the number of geodesic routes that originate in each node/agent with which José David Cabello Rondón direct and immediately interacts.

Table 12. Number of geodesic routes that originate from each node/agent that acts as a "second" in the geodesic route that connects José David Cabello Rondón with Nicolás Maduro.

Node/agent that interacts directly with José David Cabello Rondón, as "second" in the geodesic route	Number of routes that connect with Nicolás Maduro	%
César Augusto Febres Cabello	216,050	77.5067
Diosdado Cabello Rondón	23,004	8.2526
Néstor Luis Reverol Torres	14,266	5.1178
Hugo Rafael Chávez Frías	11,626	4.1708
Ramon Rafael Campos Cabello	5,899	2.1162
Benito Raúl Pereda Cordero	3,606	1.2936
Isidro Ubaldo Rondón Torres	1,532	0.5496
Ramón Alonzo Carrizález Rengifo	1,478	0.5302
José Ángel González Espín	1,284	0.4606
Sergio Alejandro Silvio Prato	3	0.0011
Marleny Josefina Contreras De Cabello	1	0.0004
Nicolás Maduro Moros	1	0.0004

As observed in Table 12, 77.5% out of the 278,750 geodesic routes that link José David Cabello Rondón with Nicolás Maduro, originate in the intermediary node/agent César Augusto Febres Cabello. This means that most of the resources that flow from José David Cabello Rondón to Nicolás Maduro have been managed through his cousin César Augusto Febres Cabello, whom he appointed in 2013 as National Intendant of Customs at the National Integrated Service for the Administration of Customs Duties and Taxes (SENIAT), and who graduated from the Military Academy of Venezuela along with Ramón Rafael Campos Cabello, his other cousin. César Augusto Febres Cabello had also been linked in 2001 to the General Services Directorate of the Ministry of the Office of the Presidency by his other cousin, José David Cabello Rondón, and currently holds management positions in state companies such as Industria Venezolana de Cemento (INVECEM), Venezolana de Cementos S.A.C.A. and Empresa de Distribución de Productos e Insumos-Venezuela Productiva, C.A. (Poderopedia, 2020).

That said, in 12.7% out of the 216,050 routes managed by César Augusto Febres Cabello as the second intermediary node/agent, the route continues with Jorge Alberto Arreaza Montserrat as the third intermediary agent, who has held positions of the highest level since Chávez's government, and with whom he shared a family bond after marrying Rosa Virginia Chávez, Chávez's eldest daughter. Currently sanctioned by the United States government for money laundering (US Department of the Treasury, 2019), Arreaza has been Minister of University Education, Science and Technology, Vice President for the Social Area, representative to the United Nations, and Minister of Foreign Affairs.

On the other hand, it is striking that 87% out of the routes that originate from César Augusto Febres Cabello, continue with Diosdado Cabello Rondón as the third intermediary node/agent, thus reinforcing a family circle centered around relatives of Diosdado Cabello that manages financial, political, and social resources. In fact, the National Integrated Service for the Administration of Customs Duties and Taxes (SENIAT) has registered the appointment of 12 members of the Cabello family who hold management positions and have some family ties with César Augusto Febres Cabello: *"Milagros Cabello Rondón (sister), Lisbeth Cabello Rondón (sister), Rafael Ernesto Contreras (brother-in-law), César Augusto Febres Cabello (cousin), Rocío Febres Cabello (cousin), Doris Febres Cabello (cousin), Blanca Pereda de Cabello (wife), Benito Raúl Pereda (brother-in-law), David Diosdado Cabello Contreras (nephew), as well as Octavio Cabello, Érika Cabello Cadena and José Manuel Cabello, make up the family map of José David Cabello in the national tax administration."* (Poderopedia, 2020).

The analysis of the first 3 nodes/agents that participate in the most relevant routes, that connect José David Cabello Rondón with Nicolás Maduro, allows inferring the operation of kleptocratic structures that are permanently reproduced in key institutional positions of the Venezuelan State. Additionally, the participation of a specific family group around Diosdado Cabello in the management of an entity such as the National Integrated Service for the Administration of Customs Duties and Taxes (SENIAT) allows inferring that this kleptocratic regime is sustained, to some extent, by a pronounced nepotism. The core of Diosdado Cabello, as well as other nuclei of nepotism that operate in the super network of macro-corruption and institutional co-optation in Venezuela, maintains the flow of resources circulating among a reduced set of nodes/agents that share family and illicit interests. These nodes/agents, located in strategic positions of the Venezuelan State, assure that economic, institutional, and political resources do not flow equitably to all sectors of the Venezuelan society. Unsurprisingly, most Venezuelans currently lack access to basic goods and social services, from food to medicine.

V. The Magnitude: the Super Network of Corruption in Venezuela Compared to *Lava Jato*

As discussed in the introduction, it is likely that the corruption registered in Venezuela during the last two decades has no historical or geographical comparison, especially when considering (i) the magnitude of the public budget from oil revenues that has been illegally appropriated, (ii) the complexity of the criminal network that sustains this process of macro-corruption and institutional co-optation, and (iii) the effects in terms of the resulting economic, social, institutional, and human damages. This chapter discusses how these characteristics make the process of macro-corruption and institutional co-optation in Venezuela exceptional.

Oil revenues have been the main object of systemic corruption during the Chávez and Maduro administrations in Venezuela; revenues that could reach up to USD$700 billion since the arrival of Chávez until 2014, according to Rafael Ramírez, former director of PDVSA, who was a collaborator of Chavism and now remains in exile (INFOBAE, 2019). As a result of the opacity promoted and even legalized in Venezuela, it is currently impossible to determine the exact amounts of oil revenue that the Venezuelan Government has squandered during the Chávez and Maduro administrations. However, the already scandalous approximations worsen when compared with amounts affected in other transnational macro-corruption schemes, such as the *Lava Jato* case.

Protocols of criminal networks analysis have been used to understand illicit macro-networks in which large numbers of individuals and organizations converge to establish numerous and diverse interactions. For example, these protocols have allowed identifying structural characteristics of a macro-corruption and institutional co-option network that nourished one of the most complex cases of transnational corruption: *Lava Jato* (Garay Salamanca, Salcedo-Albarán, & Macias, 2018d). Considering that the same analysis protocols were applied, this chapter compares the characteristics of the macro-corruption and institutional co-optation networks modeled for *Lava Jato* and Venezuela.

Although it originated in Brazil with companies that formed a cartel that called itself "El Club", to manipulate and monopolize public contracts, the *Lava Jato* macro-corruption network extended to 10 countries in Latin America and 2 in Africa (Garay Salamanca, Salcedo-Albarán, & Macías, 2018d). The *Lava Jato* scandal has reproduced political crises that, to a greater or lesser extent, involved presidents, businessmen and high-level officials in each country. For instance, in Peru, where the greatest judicial advances have been recorded outside of Brazil against public officials accused of corruption associated with *Lava Jato*, three of the last four presidents are under investigation and even serving preventive detention. Alan García, the only one of the four presidents who in 2020 did not face an investigation, committed suicide on April 17, 2019, when the authorities ordered preventive detention against him for acts of corruption related to *Lava Jato* (BBC News editorial World, 2019).

According to mid-2019 calculations, the amounts of bribes that Brazilian companies cartelized in *Lava Jato* paid to high-level public officials and candidates in Latin America amounted to more than USD$800 million (Shiel & Chavkin, 2019). These bribes included irregular contributions to political campaigns, intended to "buy" favors of those promoted and elected officials for future tenders in which the "Club" of companies would participate.

Although private agents paid bribes to public officials and funded irregular contributions to electoral campaigns in the context of *Lava Jato*, these bribes or "extra costs" were always added as cost overruns to the values of the contracts during public tender. This means that, in practice, each country paid the bribes from its own public budget as hidden additional costs. Therefore, in the absence of bribes and in a public procurement environment governed by free competition, *ceteris paribus*, each country would have paid less for the execution of the public works that were awarded through bribes. Thus, although the bribe payments are not directly extracted from the public budget, these are cost overruns that ultimately always affect each country's society. In fact, given that the society of each country must bear the economic losses derived from public tenders awarded because of bribes, the society as a whole is therefore usually the victim of corruption, which is discussed in the next chapter.

Considering the above, various Latin American countries enriched a few businessmen and public officials in at least about USD$800 million during the last decade in the context of *Lava Jato*, an amount that exceeds the bribes paid in any other previously analyzed corruption case. However, this amount is not necessarily the total of the illicit enrichment achieved by the companies involved in *Lava Jato*, nor the maximum amount of public budget losses in these affected countries. The total amounts are higher because often the companies involved did not fully deliver the works contracted despite their included cost overruns, or they did so with extended deadlines and contractual conditions better than those initially agreed at the beginning of the project. Bearing these difficulties in mind, the analysis of the social, collective and individual damages caused in the context of *Lava Jato* in each country is still a pending task.

Although the total amount of the public budget affected due to *Lava Jato* has not been calculated, if it had reached, for example, 10 times the amount of paid bribes – approximately USD$8 billion – it would still be less than the public budget potentially lost in the context of the macro-corruption and institutional co-optation process in Venezuela during the last two decades: between US$175 and US$225 billion from Chávez's arrival up until 2006, according to Coronel (2006), or approximately USD$700 billion until 2014 (INFOBAE, 2019).

If the amount of squandered public budget in Venezuela during the first two decades of this century had reached USD$700 billion, then it would be equivalent to approximately 875 times the total amount of bribes paid during *Lava Jato* throughout Latin America. Of course, these speculative calculations do not represent an accurate assessment due to the absence of objective public data in Venezuela. However, it illustrates the enormous difference in terms of magnitudes potentially affected during *Lava Jato*, and the extent of public budget potentially appropriated during

Venezuela's process of macro-corruption and institutional co-optation.

For example, in one of the multiple cases of corruption and money laundering considered when modeling this super network, brought against Venezuelan citizens in the United States' Southern District of Florida, the Prosecutor's Office has argued the illicit extraction of USD$1.2 billion of PDVSA's budget through manipulation of preferential exchange rates in 2013 and 2014. In another case, also carried out in the Court of the Southern District of Florida, the amount extracted through the same preferential exchange rate manipulation scheme was approximately USD$ 2.4 billion. This means that in only two of the more than 80 judicial processes carried out around the world against Venezuelan citizens for corruption and money laundering, the compromised sum amounts to USD$3.6 billion, while the bribes paid in the context of *Lava Jato* in Latin America approximately amount to USD$800 million.

Now, the magnitude of the illegally appropriated sums is not the only characteristic that makes the Venezuelan macro-corruption exceptional; the complexity and size of its super network is also unprecedented. For example, in the first model elaborated about *Lava Jato* in Brazil, a structure made up of 906 nodes/agents that established 2,693 interactions was identified (Garay Salamanca, Salcedo-Albarán, & Macías, 2018d). In subsequent models that included the *Lava Jato* ramification to Peru, a network made up of 1,399 nodes/agents that established 3,758 interactions was identified

(Salcedo-Albarán & Garay-Salamanca, 2019). This means that not even the *Lava Jato* macro-network of corruption and institutional co-optation extended to Brazil and Peru reaches a similar magnitude to that of Venezuela: with over 5,000 nodes/agents and over 17,000 established interactions. In fact, the super-network of macro-corruption and institutional co-optation in Venezuela exceeds by almost four times the number of nodes/agents identified in the *Lava Jato* macro-network in Brazil and Peru.

When the *Lava Jato* macro-network in Brazil and Peru was modeled, it was defined as the most extensive and complex network analyzed, due to the high numbers of nodes/agents, interactions, and countries involved (Garay Salamanca, Salcedo-Albarán, & Macías, 2018d). However, it can be noted that the analyzed super network of macro-corruption and institutional co-optation in Venezuela is, and will likely be, a regrettable global reference for a macro-corruption and systemic institutional co-optation process in any country.

VI. Human Rights Violations and Victims

As discussed in the previous chapter, the complexity of the super-network of macro-corruption and institutional co-optation in Venezuela lacks precedents in terms of (i) size and diversity, (ii) magnitude of affected public budget, and (iii) its perverse institutional and humanitarian effects. This complexity also poses unprecedented challenges in terms of the institutional, legal, and regulatory tools that will be required to address the problem. This chapter discusses some of those challenges and their resolution at the social, political, and institutional spheres, with the aim to consolidate a real democracy based on the rule of law, truth, and reparation.

Macro-corruption, Impunity, and Human Rights Violations

Although the magnitude of the public budget illegally appropriated in Venezuela possibly exceeds that of any other case, the humanitarian effects registered in this country are perhaps the main characteristic that makes this a unique case of macro-corruption and institutional co-optation in the world. For example, as previously noted in the analysis of the *Lava Jato* network in Brazil (Salcedo-Albarán, Garay-Salamanca, Macías, & Santos, 2018h) or in Peru (Salcedo-Albarán, Garay-Salamanca *et al*, 2019), no explicit interactions neither a subnetwork of human rights violations were identified as those analyzed in the case of Venezuela (Figure 5). That is, in the most complex corruption case known before Venezuela, *Lava Jato*, no interactions were identified that reported human victimization on an individual or collective scale, in terms of forced disappearances, arbitrary detentions, torture or rapes, such as the ones that multilateral organizations have documented in Venezuela. In fact, in the context of *Lava Jato*, an economic or humanitarian crisis like the ones that occurred in Venezuela has not been observed either.[3]

Although this book's main goal is not to demonstrate the causal relationship between the acts of corruption that occurred and the systematic violation of human, civil and political rights in Venezuela, it is important to point out that many of these violations have occurred within the framework of the process of institutional co-optation and reconfiguration that characterizes the macro-corruption resulting of the super network. In fact, as the United Nations has recognized with its Independent International Fact-finding Mission on the Bolivarian Republic of Venezuela (IIFFMBRV): *"An element of the crisis in Venezuela, meriting deeper investigation, is the nexus between corruption and serious human rights violations. A number of sources with whom the Mission spoke, all current or former Government or military personnel, have indicated that a motivating factor behind the human rights violations (…) are the personal financial benefits derived from the capture of State institutions, providing a strong incentive for Government actors*

---

[3] The absence of human victims identified in the *Lava Jato* network does not necessarily imply that these victims have not existed. It only implies that it is possible that there were not such direct and massive individual and collective victims in the *Lava Jato* case as those that have been registered in the macro-corruption process in Venezuela. This clarification is important because, strictly speaking, acts of corruption almost always produce human victims. However, as these victims are usually functionally, spatially and temporally distant from their perpetrators, the causal link between victims and perpetrators tends to be diffuse (Salcedo-Albarán, Zuleta, de Leon, & Rubio, 2008).

to maintain power and ensure impunity" (Human Rights Council, 2020, p. 27).

As the Maduro regime promotes enduring co-optation and reconfiguration of institutions through exacerbated clientelism and nepotism, which intensifies the illicit and massive appropriation of public resources, it is expected that the institutional functioning of the State will not only be weaken but also further distorted and reconfigured. One of the main consequences is, therefore, the impossibility of imparting impartial and expeditious justice, since the justice system tends to become an additional instrument to reproduce and deepen the institutional co-optation promoted by the regime; in other words, impunity tends to be increasingly structural and permanent, to the point of distorting the rule of law.

Under this scenario of structural impunity, individual, collective, and social violations of human rights are not attended to, prevented, or punished properly and promptly. It is not surprising that the systematic violation of individual, collective and social rights is generalized progressively promoted even from the institutional instances initially arranged to prevent and punish these violations. Therefore, the systematic violation of human rights and the deterioration of social and economic spheres are, simultaneously, cause and consequence of the profound institutional cooptation registered. In fact, even the United Nations point out that the high rates of violent deaths currently registered are part of the dynamic that links *"a weak rule of law, corruption, inequality, poverty and lack of opportunities*" (Human Rights Council, 2020, p. 198).

The dimension and complexity of the super-network of macro-corruption and institutional co-optation in Venezuela imply that the corruption process of the last two decades is systemic, that is, lasting, permanent, and reproduced by a structural system, installed in the core of the State, like the one illustrated in the third chapter. Furthermore, as this process translates into a systematic violation of human rights, it results on a perverse circle of (i) clientelism, (ii) nepotism, (iii) kleptocracy, (iv) co-optation, reconfiguration, and distortion of institutions, (v) impunity, (vi) systematic violation of individual, collective and social rights, and (vii) weakening the democratic system and the rule of law, which in turns increase the conditions for an accentuated (i) clientelism, (ii) nepotism, *etcetera*.

The systematic nature of human rights violations is manifested in structural patterns, modus operandi, and illicit practices. In other words, at this stage, human rights violations are not sporadic, but rather a cause and consequence of a system of macro-corruption and institutional co-optation, established to achieve long-term selfish and illicit objectives and orchestrated by agents of the regime with outstanding decision-making power. As a result, in Venezuela most of the human rights violations recorded "*were committed as part of a widespread and systematic attack directed against a civilian population, with knowledge of the attack, pursuant to or in furtherance of a State policy"* (Human Rights Council, 2020, p. 403). In fact, the IIFFMBRV identified patterns of human rights violations committed by some State officials or agents in at least 2,891 cases that correspond to *"extrajudicial executions, enforced disappearances, arbitrary detentions and torture and other cruel, inhumane or degrading treatment since 2014"* (Human Rights Council, 2020, p. 2).

Even under conditions of relative institutional stability, the systemic and massive nature of human rights violations would pose immense challenges to reconstruct the historical, social, and judicial truth, and to apply a necessary restorative justice. However, in Venezuela these challenges are accentuated considering the soaring level of impunity and structural ineffectiveness of the current judicial system.

Comprehensive Reparation of Individual, Collective and Social Victims

It is usually assumed that the main victim of corruption is society, which is the holder of the public budget. That is, when someone illegally appropriate public resources, it is usually assumed that there is not an individual or a collective victim affected, but only society. To this extent, there is extensive literature in which the effects of corruption on society are discussed, mainly at the economic (Ugur & Dasgupta, 2011; Department of International Development, 2015; Aidt, 2009; Alemu, 2012), social (Gupta & Holmquist, 2012; Chetwynd, Chetwynd, & Spector, 2003; Bhargava & Bolongaita, 2004; Ndikumana, 2006; Deininger & Mpuga, 2005) and political levels (Anderson & Tverdova, 2003; Cho & Kirwin, 2007; Chetwynd, Chetwynd, & Spector, 2003), even at national and local States (Chene, Clench, & Fagan, 2010). However, the same abundant literature does not pay attention to the effects of corruption over specific individuals and groups of the population. Considering the magnitude and wide diversity of damages inflicted by a super network of macro-corruption and institutional co-optation such as the one identified in Venezuela, and considering its close relationship with systematic human rights violations, it will be essential to recognize, evaluate and repair not only the societal damages but also, and crucially, those individual and collective damages caused.

Due to the difficulty involved in identifying, recognizing, and repairing individual victims to the extent that it will surely be required in Venezuela, this objective is usually restricted to transitional justice jurisdictions in which exceptional jurisprudential and legal provisions are adopted, to apply the best possible justice to the greatest number of victims. This is usually the case because in practice, traditional mechanisms of ordinary justice are not enough for applying justice to massive victims: "*What should be done after massive human rights violations, crimes against humanity, or genocide? This is the central question posed by transitional justice"* (Gidley, 2019).

Even considering the institutional and jurisprudential difficulties related to applying justice and repairing individual and collective victims after systematic violations of human rights, this reparation is critical element to restore and consolidate democracy in any society. One of the main perverse effects of systemic processes of corruption is the accentuated deterioration of institutional and interpersonal trust (Uslaner, 2013), both of which are necessary conditions for proper democratic functioning (Salcedo-Albarán, Garay-Salamanca *et al,* 2020). In Venezuela, it can be expected that these two types of trust have been seriously affected during the last two decades; therefore, it will be necessary to reconstruct the historical and social truth of the process of macro-corruption and victimization, to vindicate and apply justice under the rule of law, and to repair the affected victims.

"Society" is an abstract entity whose legal protection is different from the protection of individual rights; however, even when corruption affects a priority public sector such as health, causing lack or inadequacy of public health services, the individual victims tend to be ignored in criminal proceedings for corruption. Therefore, it is usually assumed that after corruption processes, the only affected legal asset is a social one – the public budget –, without duly considering the effects on individual rights. This difficulty in recognizing the causality that links an offender to an individual victim of corruption is reflected – and reinforced – usually by criminal codes in which crimes of corruption are interpreted as unrelated to crimes that threaten life. In fact, even under exceptional justice jurisdictions such as those of transnational justice, the humanitarian effects caused by acts of corruption also tend to be omitted, so that *"the prevailing assumption seems to be that truth commissions, human rights trials and reparation programs are aimed primarily, though not exclusively, at violations of civil and political rights that involve personal integrity or liberty, and not at violations of economic and social rights, including large-scale corruption crimes and plunder"* (Carranza, 2008, p. 310).

Due to the abstract nature of society as a legal entity, repairing its damages requires different acts of compensation than those required to repair individuals and groups. In this sense, comprehensive reparation for victims of corruption must include the recognition of individual, collective and social damages, in both patrimonial and extra-patrimonial extent. In other words, even a massive violation of human, civil and political rights of individuals cannot be grouped into the category of "social harm". As a result, States require institutional and legal mechanisms to identify and repair individual and collective damages of victims.

Now, in countries where mass victimization has happened, there are usually institutional and legal tools to achieve reparation of individual, collective, and social victims, through jurisprudence and jurisdictions that are not restricted to the transitional one. In Colombia, for instance, there are legal provisions,[4] as well as sentences of the Constitutional Court,[5] that make up a legal body that has progressively been translated into institutional designs to face the massive victimization registered during the country's internal armed conflict. Similar legal mechanisms and supports will be essential in Venezuela to identify and repair the damages of individual and collective victims in the context of the super network of macro-corruption and institutional co-optation.

As pointed out, these reparations should involve patrimonial and extra-patrimonial components, and they should be accompanied by precepts of anamnestic justice –or "memorial justice" or "justice of memory"–, since it is usually impossible to apply principles of traditional punitive justice to deal with massive numbers of victims, as it will be required in Venezuela. For this purpose, it is essential to identify those potential nodes/agents bearing the greatest responsibility in mass victimization processes.

---

[4] In Colombia, under the Law 1448 of 2011, *"(…) are considered victims (…), those persons who have suffered damage individually or collectively due to events that occurred as of January 1, 1985, as a consequence of violations of International Humanitarian Law, or of grave and manifest violations of international human rights standards, which occurred during the internal armed conflict"*.

[5] For example, the Sentence T-025 of 2004 and the numerous follow-up systematic orders on the problem of internal forced displacement that occurred in Colombia due to the internal armed conflict. The Sentence and the orders, among other effects, resulted in the approval of the Law of victims for seeking comprehensive and integral reparation of damages suffered by the victims of forced internal displacement.

Nodes/agents with the Greatest Responsibility in the Super Network

As individual and collective victims become massive during processes of advanced macro-corruption and institutional co-optation, the causal links between victims and perpetrators are easily perceived (Salcedo-Albarán *et al*, 2008). For example, if hundreds or thousands of patients lack medical treatments in Venezuela due to constant power cuts resulting of corruption in the maintenance of the country's energy infrastructure, the corrupt nodes/agents that led to this malfunction of the energy structure could be interpreted as potentially bearing the highest responsibility for violating the right to life of the affected patients.

Although the objective of this book is not to demonstrate the mediate or immediate authorship of specific nodes/agents, it is important to highlight that in cases such as Venezuela, with individual, collective, and social damages recognized by domestic and international organizations, it is increasingly evident that the nodes/agents who facilitate and articulate the super network can be interpreted as bearing great responsibility of those damages. In this case, the greatest responsibility could be partially inferred by identifying, for example, high indicators of direct centrality and capacity for intervention (betweenness), such as those discussed in the third chapter of the book. Something similar could be argued about the nodes/agents that register high indicators in the subnetworks, as potentially responsible for the specific objectives of each subnetwork.

Regarding the human rights violations analyzed by the IIFFMBRV, *"the Mission has information indicating that the President and the Ministers of Interior and of Defense were aware of the crimes. They were in close contact with other members of the FANB, including the GNB, and also with the Directors of the PNB, CICPC, SEBIN and DGCIM"* (Human Rights Council, 2020, p. 406). Observations like this one coincide with the fact that Nicolás Maduro probably bears a great responsibility according to the concentration of direct interactions (direct centrality indicator) and the ability to intervene in the resource flows (betweenness) in the subnetworks and the super network.

The indicators of direct centrality and capacity for intervention analyzed herein do not constitute a sufficient criterion to irrefutably point out the most responsible nodes/agents in the processes of massive human rights violations. However, these elements indicate which nodes/agents have been decisive to articulate the subnetworks and the macro-network. Thus, considering that the results of the model analyzed herein coincide with the findings of the IIFFMBRV regarding the potential criminal responsibility of those holding key decision-making positions in the Venezuelan government, the judicial imputation of these relevant agents will require an exhaustive judicial analysis, since *"(t)he violations and crimes documented in this report give rise to individual criminal responsibility, either under domestic criminal law or international criminal law, or under both"* (Human Rights Council, 2020, p. 402).

It is therefore critical to identify and analyze those nodes/agents bearing the greatest responsibility in macro-corruption and institutional co-optation networks such as the one analyzed herein, because in the face of systematic human rights violations, the potential application of justice cannot be restricted solely to the immediate perpetrators who execute the crimes but also to those "behind them" – the so-called mediate perpetrators–, holding decision making positions. In this sense, applying justice in Venezuela in the context of massive and systematic human rights violations, will require identifying and investigating those nodes/agents that have promoted illicit and criminal objectives and articulated the super network or its subnetworks. Regarding this objective, it has been recognized that officials in high decision-making positions, have instructed and provided resources to promote human rights violations (Human Rights Council, 2020).

Clarifying levels of responsibility is particularly important considering that in the few cases in which the Venezuelan justice system initiated judicial investigations and prosecutions regarding human rights violations, *"(…) these proceedings did not ensure the accountability of immediate superiors, or those higher up in the chain of command (…). In many cases, also, accountability did not cover all but some of the crimes committed against the given individuals. In the vast majority of cases, the violations and crimes documented in this report were met with impunity and inaction by the responsible authorities"* (Human Rights Council, 2020, p. 436).

Heterodox Justice to Confront the Super Network

The systematic violation of human rights and the consequent individual, collective and social damages observed in Venezuela, make this process similar to those observed in countries that experience economic, political, social and humanitarian crisis as a result of authoritarian regimes such as dictatorships, or of the reconfiguration of key state instances by powerful illegal and illegitimate individuals and groups.

The process of macro-corruption and institutional co-optation observed in Venezuela during the last two decades is characterized by (i) systemic corruption in the management of high revenues resulting of exploitation of oil, hydrocarbons, and minerals, (ii) a convergence of nodes/agents – even some strictly criminal – who co-opt and reconfigure instances of public institutions, and (iii) a severe political, social, and economic emergency. Therefore, the institutional mechanisms required to deal with this situation should contemplate ambitious structural transformations in various areas, in addition to effectively implant jurisprudence and legal tools that most domestic jurisdictions in Latin America do not have today. For this reason, organizations such as Transparencia Venezuela have emphasized the need to design and adopt heterodox justice systems when the political conditions be the right ones (Transparencia Venezuela, 2019).

When the political conditions allow the institutional and democratic construction of the Venezuelan State, it will be necessary to adequately judge those agents responsible of the process of macro-corruption and massive victimization, as well as to identify and repair the victims to re-establish the minimum levels of interpersonal and institutional trust required for citizen coexistence in a functional democratic society (Ohbuchi, Kameda, & Agarie, 1989; Sharp, 2007; Bachmann, Gillespie, & Priem, 2015). Without adequate levels of trust, it will be impossible to properly restore the notion of social order (Dirks, Lewicki, & Zaheer, 2009).

In the American continent, under normal conditions, nor ordinary jurisdiction of justice can clarify each fact that conforms a process of macro-corruption, institutional co-optation, and violation of human rights as complex as the one happening in Venezuela. For this reason, innovative instruments and legal figures will be required for the process of institutional and democratic construction.

Traditionally, the objectives of reconstructing social memory and truth, repairing victims, and securing the non-repetition of victimization have been restricted to transitional justice jurisdictions, designed for crimes against humanity that occurred under dictatorial regimes and wars (Gamboa, 2007; Diaz, 2018). On the opposite, the application of justice to clarify and prosecute acts of corruption has usually been approached through ordinary justice jurisdictions without the explicit purpose of reconstructing social and historical truth or repairing victims. However, considering the effects of mass victimization derived from macro-corruption and institutional co-optation processes such as those analyzed herein, it will be impossible to evade the application of principles of justice, especially those anamnestic and restorative (Johnstone & W., 2007), as a condition to establish democratic institutions in Venezuela; this is a *sine qua non* for securing an inclusive, democratic and prosperous society, in accordance with its natural, human, economic and social potential.

VII. *Post scriptum*: Comprehensive Reparation for Victims of Corruption in the Health Sector

Considering the importance of recognizing, calculating, and carrying out the corresponding integral reparation of damages caused, Garay-Salamanca, Salcedo-Albarán, & Vanegas (2020) proposed a comprehensive reparation matrix to guide this process in the case of the health sector. This proposal is part of the analysis of a case of macro-corruption process in the provision of specialized and high-cost medical treatments to hemophilia patients in Colombia (Garay Salamanca, Salcedo-Albarán, & Álvarez Villa, 2020). As shown in Table 13, this matrix includes actions specifically aimed at remedying victims who did not receive medical treatments provided by the public health system due to processes of macro-corruption and institutional co-optation.

When proposing integral reparation for victims of macro-corruption and institutional co-optation processes, one of the main institutional and legal challenges is to estimate the individual and collective damages derived from the illicit acts committed by perpetrators. For this reason, the following matrix includes those minimum elements to be considered when calculating individual damages (Garay-Salamanca, Salcedo-Albarán, & Vanegas, 2020):

- Cost of rehabilitation after the lack of medical treatment for primary illness (Ceo).

- Cost of rehabilitation and care of secondary effects derived from the initial lack of medical treatment (Ces).

- Emergent individual damage + updated loss of earnings of income not received due to the original untreated illness, as well as secondary illness and effects derived from the initial of lack medical attention (DiEmLc).

- Transformative reparation of the initial or previous vulnerable conditions (Rt).

- Increase of irreversible damage to the patient's functional motor quality due to hemarthrosis (Δdm).

- Increase of bleeding risk in the central nervous, respiratory, gastrointestinal, and intra-ocular systems, as well as abdominal tracts (Δrh).

These elements are expressed in the following formula:

RiP (Individual patrimonial reparation) = [CEo + CEs + DiEmLc + Rt] * (1 + Δdm) * (1 + Δrh).

Additionally, the following are those minimum elements to be considered when repairing collective damages to the group of hemophilia patients (Garay-Salamanca, Salcedo-Albarán, & Vanegas, 2020, p. 81):

- Cost of research projects to increase knowledge about the disease (Cit).

- Cost of restructuring and optimizing the care system for patients with the disease (Coa).

- Number of HA patients who have been victimized (PvHA).

- Total estimated number of HA patients in the department, state or province (PvHA).

These elements are expressed in the following formula:

RcP (Collective patrimonial reparation) = [(Cit+Coa) * (1+ (PvHA/PHA)].

As these elements conform the potential integral reparation of damages caused to victims who are Hemophilia patient due to lack of medical attention, other diseases with high-cost treatments are constantly scenario for macro-corruption and institutional co-optation, such as HIV and Down syndrome, as well as assistance programs for the elderly (Garay-Salamanca, Salcedo-Albarán, & Vanegas, 2020).

Regarding Venezuela, it is important to define more complex calculations than those proposed above, to define comprehensive and integral reparation – at individual, collective and social levels – to patients with other diseases. In fact, comprehensive reparation for victims of corruption in the Venezuelan health sector should also consider those who have been harmed by the shortage of medicines (Center for Development Studies, Central University of Venezuela, 2016), by the deterioration of the hospital network (Doctors for health, 2020), and even by illnesses with less complex treatments but whose current indicators reflect a high incidence among the population, such as malaria (Pan American Health Organization and World Health Organization, 2020).

Table 13. Comprehensive and integral reparation matrix. (Garay-Salamanca, Salcedo-Albarán, & Vanegas, 2020, p. 83).

	Individual reparation (Ir)	Collective reparation (Cr)	Social reparation (Sr)
Patrimonial	RiP: -Rehabilitating the patient due to the progression of the original disease, when possible. -Paying at least one caring person for the patient affected by the progression of the original disease and by the secondary diseases. -Rehabilitating the patient for secondary diseases, derived from the absence of the original disease. -Improving living conditions of the victims and their families, ensuring their social care from the State or a private health provider. -Paying consequential damages, and lost earnings from income not received due to reasons of the original disease not being treated, as well as secondary effects.	RcP: -Funding special programs to secure optimal care for the group of patients. -Funding research programs to improve understanding and care of diseases that affect the community.	RsP: -Paying to the local, regional, and national State for the emergent damage and the updated lost earnings, derived from affected amounts, originally oriented to finance the health care system.

Extra patrimonial/ moral	RiExp: -Issuing personal letters of apology. -Including the information in truth commission reports. -Naming streets and public places, after the victim. -Funding the compensation according to the legislation.	RcExp: -Updating the census of potential patients that conform the group of victims. -Celebrating public events honoring the group of patients/victims. -Establishing museums or cultural activities that vindicate the resilience of the affected group. -Naming streets or public places where the victimizing events occurred, after some of the victims. -Disclosing information to prevent the repetition of collective victimization.	RsExp: -Issuing public apologies to the local, regional, and national State. -Securing non-repetition of the victimizing acts, through institutional or legislative arrangements. - Securing the control, prevention, and punishment of the acts of corruption.

Bibliography

ACNUR. (2019, Jun. 07). *Refugiados y migrantes de Venezuela superan los cuatro millones: ACNUR y OIM*. Retrieved from ACNUR.ORG: https://www.acnur.org/noticias/press/ 2019/6/5cfa5eb64/refugiados-y-migrantes-de-venezuela-superan-los-cuatro-millones-acnur-y.html

Aidt, T. (2009). Corruption, Institutions, and Economic Development. *Oxford Review of Economic Policy, 25*(2), 271-291.

Alemu, A. M. (2012). Effects of Corruption on FDI Inflow in Asian Economies. *Seoul Journal of Economics, 25*(4), 387-412.

Amnistía Internacional. (2018). *Informe Amnistía Internacional: La Situación de los Derechos Humanos en el Mundo*. London: Amnistía Internacional. Retrieved from Amnistia Internacional: https://www.amnesty.org/es/countries/ americas/venezuela/report-venezuela/

Anderson, C. J., & Tverdova, Y. V. (2003, Jan.). Corruption, Political Allegiances, and Attitudes Toward Government in Contemporary Democracies. *American Journal of Political Science, 47*(1), 91-109.

Bachmann, R., Gillespie, N., & Priem, R. (2015). Repairing Trust in Organizations and Institutions: Toward a Conceptual Framework. *Organization Studies, 36*(9), 1123 - 1142.

Bhargava, V., & Bolongaita, E. (2004). *Challenging Corruption in Asia: Case Studies and a Framework for Action*. World Bank. Washington, D.C.: World Bank.

Borgatti, S. P., Mehra, A., Brass, D., & Labianca, G. (2009). Network Analysis in the Social Sciences. *Science, 323*, 892-895.

Carranza, R. (2008). Plunder and Pain: Should Transitional Justice Engage with Corruption and Economic Crimes? *The International Journal of Transitional Justice, 2*, 310-330.

Carrington, P. J., Scoot, J., & Wasserman, S. (2005). *Models and Methods in Social Network Analysis.* New York: Cambridge University Press.

Centro de Estudios del Desarrollo, Universidad Central de Venezuela. (2016). *Crisis en la disponibilidad de insumos de salud.* Retrieved from Observatorio Venezolano de la Salud: https://www.ovsalud.org/boletines/salud/crisis-disponibilidad-insumos-salud/

Chetwynd, E., Chetwynd, F., & Spector, B. (2003). *Corruption and Poverty: A Review of Recent Literature.* London: Management Systems International.

Chêne, M., Clench, B., & Fagan, C. (2010). *Corruption and Gender in Service Delivery: The Unequal Impacts.* Berlin: Transparency International.

Cho, W., & Kirwin, M. A. (2007). *Vicious Circle of Corruption and Mistrust in Institutions in Sub-Saharan Africa: A Micro-Level Analysis.* Afrobarometer Working Paper.

Human Rights Council. (2015). *Reporte del Comité Asesor del Human Rights Council sobre las consecuencias negativas de la corrupción en el disfrute de los derechos humanos.* New York: Naciones Unidas.

Human Rights Council. (2020). *Conclusiones detalladas de la Misión internacional independiente de determinación de los hechos sobre la República Bolivariana de Venezuela.* New York: Naciones Unidas.

Coronel, G. (2006). *Corruption, Mismanagement, and Abuse of Power in Hugo Chávez's Venezuela.* CATO Institute.

Csermely, P. (2006). *Weak Links: Stabilizers ofComplex Systems from Proteins to Social Networks.* New York: Springer-Verlag.

Degenne, A., & Forsé, M. (1999). *Introducing Social Networks.* London: SAGE Publications.

Deininger, K., & Mpuga, P. (2005). Does Greater Accountability Improve the Quality of Public Service Delivery? Evidence from Uganda. *World Development, 33*(1), 222-239.

Delgado, A. M. (2020, Jul 14). *Cape Verde approves extradition to U.S. of Venezuelan regime's financial whiz.* Retrieved from Miami Herald: https://www.miamiherald.com/news/nation-world/world/americas/venezuela/article244212727.html

Department of International Development. (2015). *Why corruption matters: understanding causes, effects and how to address them.* Department of International Development & UKAid. London: Department of International Development & UKAid.

Diaz, F. A. (2018). *Truth, Justice and Reconciliation in Colombia: Transitioning from Violence.* New York: Routledge.

Dirks, K., Lewicki, R., & Zaheer, A. (2009). Repairing relationships within and between organizations: Building a conceptual foundation. *Academy of Management Review, 34*(1), 68 - 84.

Dunbar, R. (1998). *Grooming, Gossip, and the Evolution of Language.* Harvard University Press.

El País. (2019, Apr. 16). *Venezuela sufre el mayor aumento de casos de malaria del mundo.* Retrieved from El País: https://elpais.com/elpais/2019/04/16/planeta_futuro/1555402255_653709.html

Fundación Vortex. (2020b). *Propuesta metodológica para identificar redes y patrones de macro- corrupción por parte de la Procuraduría General de la Nación.* Bogotá: Fundación Vortex.

Gamboa, J. C. (2007). *Seeking Integral Reparations for the Murders and Disappearances of Women in Ciudad Juárez: A Gender and Cultural Perspective.* Human Rights Brief 14.

Garay Salamanca, L. J., & Salcedo-Albarán, E. (2012). *Narcotráfico, Corrupción y Estados: Cómo las redes ilícitas han reconfigurado las instituciones de Colombia, Guatemala y México.* Ciudad de México: Random House Mondadori.

Garay Salamanca, L. J., Salcedo-Albaran, E., & Álvarez Villa, D. (2020). *Macro-Corrupción y Cooptación Institucional en el departamento de Córdoba, Colombia.* Bogotá: Fedesarrollo.

Garay Salamanca, L., Salcedo-Albarán, E., & Macías, G. (2018d). *Macro-Corruption and Institutional Co-optation: The "Lava Jato" Criminal Network.* Bogotá, Colombia: Fundación Vortex.

Garay-Salamanca, L. J., & Salcedo-Albarán, E. (2012a, March). Institutional Impact of Criminal Networks in Colombia and Mexico. *Crime, Law and Social Change, 57*(2), 177-194.

Garay-Salamanca, L. J., Salcedo-Albarán, E., & Duarte, N. (2017). *Elenopolítica: Reconfiguración cooptada del Estado en Arauca, Colombia.* Bogotá: Fundación Vortex.

Garay-Salamanca, L. J., Salcedo-Albaran, E., & Vanegas, S. (2020). Los daños causados por corrupción sistémica: Líneamientos para contextos de redes de macrocorrupción, de cooptación institucional y de "gran corrupción" en Colombia. In Transparencia por Colombia, *La reparación de las víctimas de la corrupción en Colombia: Enfoque, exploración de ruta jurídica y elementos para una metodología de tasación* (pp. 45-62). Bogotá: Transparencia por Colombia.

Garay-Salamanca, L., Salcedo-Albarán, E., & Beltrán, I. (2010a). Redes de poder en Casanare y la Costa Atlántica. In C. López, *Y Refundaron la Patria: De cómo mafiosos y políticos reconfiguraron el estado colombiano* (pp. 251 - 302). Bogotá: Random House Mondadori.

Garay-Salamanca, L., Salcedo-Albarán, E., & Beltrán, I. (2010b). *Illicit Networks Reconfiguring States: Social Network Analysis of Colombian and Mexican Cases.* Bogotá: Método.

Garcia, J., Correa, G., & Rousset, B. (2019). Trends in infant mortality in Venezuela between 1985 and 2016: a systematic analysis of demographic data. *Lancet Glob Health, 7*, e331–36.

Bibliography

Gidley, R. (2019). *Illiberal Transitional Justice and the Extraordinary Chambers in the Courts of Cambodia*. Cham: Palgrave Macmillan.

Global Networks Against Food Crisis & Food Security Information Network. (2020). *Global Report on Food Crisis 2020: Joint Analysis for Better Decisions*. New York: WFP.

Goga, K., G. C., & Salcedo-Albaran, E. (2017). *The Rhino Horn Trafficking Network of the Groenewald Gang*. Bogota: Vortex Foundation.

Gupta, S., & Holmquist, F. (2012). Reform and Political Impunity in Kenya: Transparency without Accountability. *African Studies Review, 55*(1), 53-74.

Hübschle, A. (2017). *The Groenwald Criminal Network*. Bogota: Vortex Foundation.

Hepp, S. (2019). *The effect of declining oil prices on political corruption in Venezuela*. Tesis de maestría, Naval Posgraduate School, Monterrey, California.

Human Rights Watch. (2017). *Crackdown on Dissent Brutality: Torture, and Political Persecution in Venezuela*. Washington, D.C.: Human Rights Watch & Foro Penal.

INFOBAE. (2019, 01 19). *INFOBAE*. Retrieved from Rafael Ramírez aseguró que durante los 10 años que estuvo al frente de PDVSA se perdieron unos 700 mil millones de dólares: https://www.infobae.com/america/venezuela/2020/01/19/rafael-ramirez-aseguro-que-durante-los-10-anos-que-estuvo-al-frente-de-pdvsa-se-perdieron-unos-700-mil-millones-de-dolares/

Jácome, F. (2017). Los militares en la política y la economía de Venezuela. *Nueva sociedad*(274), 119-128.

Johnstone, G., & W., V. N. (2007). *Handbook of Restorative Justice*. New York: Routledge.

Kumar, H., Toshniwal, A., & Gupta, S. (2016). The Resource Curse Play: A Comparative Study of Norway and Venezuela. *Journal of Economics and Finance, 7*(5), 13-20.

Lander, E., & Arconada, S. (2017). Venezuela: un barril de pólvora. *Nueva sociedad*(269), 17-26.

Li, G., Hu, J., Song, Y., Yang, Y., & Li, H. (2019). Analysis of the Terrorist Organization Alliance Network Based on Complex Network Theory. *Institute of Electrical and Electronics Engineers, 7*, 103854-103862.

Lopez, E., & Salcedo-Albaran, E. (2017). *Coltan Trafficking Criminal Network in the Democratic Republic of the Congo.* Bogotá: Vortex Foundation.

López Maya, M. (2018). Populism, 21st-century socialism and corruption in Venezuela. *Thesis eleven, 149*(1), 67-83.

Médicos por la salud. (2020). *Encuesta Nacional de Hospitales 2019, Balance Final.* Caracas: Médicos por la salud.

Mejia, J. (2018). Venezuela in Crisis: A Backgrounder. *Colloquium: The Political Science Journal of Boston College, 2*(2), 42-53.

Morselli, C. (2008). *Inside Criminal Networks.* Montreal: Springer.

Morselli, C. (2012). Assessing network patterns in illegal firearm markets. *Crime Law Soc Change,* 129-149.

Mungiu-Pippidi, A. (2017). *Corruption as Social Order.* World Development Report.

Ndikumana, L. (2006). *Corruption and Pro-Poor Growth Outcomes: Evidence and Lessons for African Countries.* Amherst: University of Massachusetts.

Oficina de la Alta Comisionada de las Naciones Unidas para los Derechos Humanos. (2019). *Informe de la Alta Comisionada de las Naciones Unidas para los Derechos Humanos sobre la situación de los derechos humanos en la República Bolivariana de Venezuela.* New York: Naciones Unidas.

Ohbuchi, K., Kameda, M., & Agarie, N. (1989). Apology as aggression control: Its role in mediating appraisal of and response to harm. *Journal of Personality and Social Psychology, 56*, 219 - 227.

Olmo, G. (2020, 01 15). *Venezuela: de dónde salen los dólares que circulan en el país (y por qué se cree que ya hay más que bolívares).* Retrieved from BBC News: https://www.bbc.com/mundo/noticias-america-latina-51057901

Organización Panamericana de la Salud y Organización Mundial de la Salud. (2020). *Indicadores Básicos 2019, Tendencias de la salud en las Américas.* Organización Panamericana de la Salud.

Peters, S. (2017). Beyond curse and blessing: Rentier society in Venezuela. In B. Engels, & K. Dietz, *Contested extractivism, society and the state* (pp. 45-68). Londres: Pallgrave Macmillan.

Poderopedia. (2020, Dic 14). *César Augusto Febres Cabello.* Retrieved from PODEROPEDIA: https://poderopediave.org/persona/cesar-augusto-febres-cabello/

Puerta Riera, M. (2017). Venezuela: The decline of democracy . *Development, 60*(3-4), 174-179.

Redacción BBC News Mundo. (2019, Jul 31). *BBC News Mundo.* Retrieved from Tareck El Aissami: EE.UU. incluye al ministro de Venezuela en la lista de los 10 más buscados por narcotráfico internacional: https://www.bbc.com/mundo/noticias-america-latina-49186405

Redacción BBC News Mundo. (2019, 04 19). *BBC News Mundo.* Retrieved from Muerte de Alan García: la carta de suicidio que dejó el expresidente peruano : https://www.bbc.com/mundo/noticias-america-latina-47993238

Salcedo-Albarán, E., & Garay-Salamanca, L. (2016). *Macro-Criminalidad: Complejidad y Resiliencia de las Redes Criminales.* Bloomington: iUniverse, Vortex Foundation, Small Wars Journal.

Salcedo-Albarán, E., & Garay-Salamanca, L. J. (2019g). *Súper-estructura Lava Jato en Brasil y Perú*. Bogotá: Vortex Foundation.

Salcedo-Albaran, E., & Garay-Salamanca, L. J. (2019). *Súperestructura de corrupción Lava Jato en Brasil y Perú*. Bogotá: Vortex Foundation.

Salcedo-Albaran, E., & Santos, D. (2017). *The Medicus Case: Organ Trafficking Network*. Bogota: Vortex Foundation.

Salcedo-Albaran, E., Garay, L. J., Macias, G., & Santos, D. (2018h). *"Lava Jato": Cartelización para obtener ventajas indebidas en la contratación pública*. Bogotá: Fundación Vortex.

Salcedo-Albaran, E., Garay, L. J., Ugaz, J., de Freitas, M., & Vanegas, S. (2020). *Victims of Corruption: Integral Reparation and Institutional Trust as Cores of Anticorruption Strategies*. Bogota: Vortex Foundation.

Salcedo-Albaran, E., Garay-Salamanca, L. J., Macias, G., Velasco, G., & Pastor, C. (2019). *Lava Jato Perú*. Lima: Proética.

Salcedo-Albaran, E., Zuleta, M. M., de Leon, I., & Rubio, M. (2008). Feelings, Brain and Prevention of Corruption. *International Journal of Psychology Research, 3*(3), 173-190.

Sharp, S. (2007). The Idea of Reparation. In G. Johnstone, & W. Van Ness D., *Handbook of Restorative Justice* (pp. 23-40). New York: Routledge.

Shiel, F., & Chavkin, S. (2019, 06 25). *ICIJ*. Retrieved from Bribery Division: What is Odebrecht? Who is Involved?: https://www.icij.org/investigations/bribery-division/bribery-division-what-is-odebrecht-who-is-involved/

Sutherland, M. (2018). La ruina de Venezuela no se debe al <<socialismo>> ni a la <<revolución>>. *Nueva sociedad*(274), 142-151.

Transparencia Venezuela. (2017). *¿Crisis Humanitaria o emergencia compleja en Venezuela?* Caracas: Transparencia Venezuela.

Transparencia Venezuela. (2019). *Informe Corrupción 2018*. Caracas: Transparencia Venezuela.

Transparencia Venezuela. (2019, 05 19). *Transparencia Venezuela*. Retrieved from Es necesario construir un sistema de justicia heterodoxo con apoyo internacional para sancionar la Gran Corrupción: https://transparencia.org.ve/es-necesario-construir-un-sistema-de-justicia-heterodoxo-con-apoyo-internacional-para-sancionar-la-gran-corrupcion/

U.S. Department of the Treasury. (2017, Nov 09). *Treasury Sanctions Ten Venezuelan Government Officials*. Retrieved from U.S. Department of the Treasury - Press Center: https://www.treasury.gov/press-center/press-releases/Pages/sm0214.aspx

U.S. Department of the Treasury. (2019, Abr 26). *Treasury Sanctions Venezuelan Minister of Foreign Affairs*. Retrieved from U.S. Department of the Treasury: https://uy.usembassy.gov/treasury-sanctions-venezuelan-minister-of-foreign-affairs/

U.S. Immigration and Customs Enforcement. (2020, Ene 15). *Venezuelan attorney and businessman added to ICE Most Wanted List for conspiracy to violate the Foreign Corrupt Practices Act and money laundering*. Retrieved from U.S. Immigration and Customs Enforcement: https://www.ice.gov/news/releases/venezuelan-attorney-and-businessman-added-ice-most-wanted-list-conspiracy-violate

Ugur, M., & Dasgupta, N. (2011). *Evidence on the economic growth impacts of corruption in low-income countries and beyond: a systematic review*. London: EPPI-Centre, Social Science Research Unit, Institute of Education, University of London.

United Nations, Human Rights Office of the High Commissioner. (2018). *Human rights violations in the Bolivarian Republic of Venezuela: a downward spiral with no end in sight*. New York: United Nations.

Uslaner, E. M. (2013). Trust and corruption revisited: how and why trust and corruption shape each other. *Quality & Quantity, 47*, 3603–3608.

Vera, L. (2018). ¿Cómo explicar la catástrofe económica venezolana? *Nueva sociedad*(274), 83-96.

Vera-Licona, P., Bonnet, E., Barillot, E., & Zinovyev, A. (2013). OCSANA: optimal combinations of interventions from network analysis. *Bioinformatics, 29*(12), 1571-1573.

Vortex Foundation & SciVortex Corp. (2020). *Instructions for analyzing criminal networks - VPARC 1.0.* Saint Petersburg: Vortex Foundation & SciVortex Corp.

"Cristales I" (2017) by Luz Marina Albarán.
Oil, 76 x 61 cm.